SERGEANT YORK and the GREAT WAR

HIS OWN LIFE STORY AND WAR DIARY

Originally Edited By
Tom Skeyhill 1930

MY FATHER'S WORLD®

Published by
My Father's World®
PO Box 2140, Rolla, MO 65402
(573) 202-2000 info@mfwbooks.com
www.mfwbooks.com

May 2015

Dedicated to:
my friends,
Dr. Jim Leininger who inspired me with the vision
of joining the life of Alvin York and the inserts of the
history of World War I
and
Alvin Mendenhall whose lifetime hero was Alvin York.
While wrestling with Quaker convictions during the Vietnam War, Al
drew inspiration from the example of Alvin York and served overseas as
a chaplain's assistant.

Sergeant Alvin C. York, America's One-Man Army

Contents

Preface

The story you are about to read is a three-fold perspective of *Sergeant York and the Great War*. The first consists of primary source material from Alvin C. York's own wartime journal. The second facet involves the contemporary author, Tom Skeyhill's recorded interviews with Alvin York after the *Great War*, World War I. And for further understanding the editor has included background research.

Mr. Skeyhill took up residence in Pall Mall, Tennessee, among the mountain folk who had known Alvin and his family long before World War I took place. While living in Pall Mall, Mr. Skeyhill was able to see firsthand the manner of life of these hardy mountain people and to write about them, thus bringing the nature of Alvin York to the American people outside the remote regions of the Tennessee mountains. Mr. Skeyhill followed the adage "When in Rome, do as the Romans do," adapting to the mountain people's way of life in order to bring the truest perspective to his writing.

After World War I, this one-time relatively unknown Tennessee soldier was thrust into the annals of living history. Whether Alvin York liked it or not, his war deeds as recorded in his own writing, and classic film by portrayed by Gary Cooper, brought him national and world attention. People wanted to know all about the shy and quiet Christian soldier, who, some enthusiastically said, "captured the whole German army."

As you read *Sergeant York and the Great War*, you will find Mr. Skeyhill did not alter or correct Alvin's colloquialisms and unique style in Alvin York's personal diary, but rather left his numerous grammatical mistakes intact. For a grammarian, the reading is a nightmare, with inconsistent spelling and punctuation errors throughout the diary. For the historian like myself, it is wonderful, and draws the reader into the life of Sergeant York. You will feel as if you have walked with him and personally known him when you have finished reading this book.

Alvin had what is equivalent to a third-grade education and therefore, knew only the basics of reading and writing. Prior to the war, the only book Alvin York ever read was about the lives of Jesse and Frank James. He had little time to devote to study; just plain living took all his time in the harsh environment of the rugged mountains of northeast Tennessee along the three forks of the Wolf River.

I have taken the liberty in this book to insert rare photos of the war to illustrate what changed Sergeant York's life forever and to add details that enhance the study of the Great War that was supposed to "end all wars." Alvin York's war diary and the study of World War I is just as important today as it was many years ago. Young people continue to need exemplary role models after which to pattern their lives. And although Alvin York, has gone on to eternal glory, he left a legacy of Godly character for others to follow.

Sad to say, most Americans know very little of past heroes and America's involvement in World War I and II and subsequent wars. I have discovered that the majority of students of the sixties and seventies graduated without ever studying American history much beyond the Civil War. With that in mind, perhaps this book will be educational, as well as inspirational.

Author/Publisher/Editor,
Mantle Ministries Press
Richard "Little Bear" Wheeler

Chronology of the Major Events Surrounding Alvin C. York

December 13,1887 Alvin C. York is born to William and Mary Brooks York.

February 7,1900 Gracie Loretta Williams, Alvin's future wife, was born to Asbury and Alice Williams.

November 17,1911 Alvin's father is kicked in the chest by a mule. He dies on Christmas Day, his thirtieth wedding anniversary.

January 1912 Alvin takes full responsibility to provide for his mother and eight younger siblings, his two older brothers having already left home.

January 1, 1915 Alvin surrenders his sinful life to Christ after hearing Melvin H. Russell, a circuit-riding minister to the Church of Christ in Christian Union. He was already being influenced by the teachings of Pastor R. C. Pile, the minister of the Church of Christ.

1916 Alvin earns $1.60 per day building roads and farming.

April 6, 1917 United States declares war on Germany.

June 5, 1917 York receives his induction notice.

August 28, 1917 York submits the request to be exempt from military service due to religious convictions.

October 5, 1917 District draft board denies the request.

October 28, 1917 Alvin walks twelve miles to receive

physical examination for military service. (He weighs in at 170 pounds and measures seventy-two inches tall.) He is approved for military duty.

November 14, 1917 Alvin York says farewell to family, friends, and future wife, Gracie Williams. He heads for Camp Gordon, Georgia, where he is registered as Private Alvin C. York, Serial number 1910421, and assigned to the 21st Training Battalion.

February 1918 He is assigned to Company G, 328th Battalion 1st Platoon, 82nd Division (the All-American Division). Company commander Major George Buxton and Captain E. C. B. Danforth.

March 29, 1918 York receives leave for several days to decide whether or not, as a Christian, he should proceed and go overseas to fight as a Christian.

April 19, 1918 York leaves Georgia for Camp Upton, New York, before transferring overseas.

May 1, 1918 York boards a Scandinavian troop transport in Boston and heads for England.

May 16, 1918 He arrives in Liverpool, England.

May 21, 1918 He leaves Southampton, England, for French shores.

October 8, 1918 York performs his amazing feat over the Germans on Hill 223.

October 8, 1918 York is promoted from Corporal to Sergeant.

February 3, 1919 Brigadier General Lindsey and Major Buxton interview York on location at Hill 223 to have him review the details of the famous battle.

February 11, 1919 York receives the American Distinguished Service Cross during review in front of General Blackjack Pershing. General Pershing attaching the medal, says to York, "You are the greatest civilian soldier of the war."

April 8, 1919 York is on hand at the Palace of Versailles, Paris, France, to witness the signing of the peace treaty. York is personally introduced to Premier Clemenceau and Marshal Foch.

April 18, 1919 Good Friday, Alvin York receives the Congressional Medal of Honor at St. Silva, France, by divisional commander Major General George B. Duncan.

May 10, 1919 York boards the ship *USS Ohio* and heads for the USA, arriving May 22, 1919.

May 25- May 28,1919 Alvin York was offered a total of $185,000 dollars in various contracts to promote himself and tell his war story to the American people. He turned down all offers, only wanting to return to his peaceful way of living. He did not feel right selling "Uncle Sam's" uniform.

May 29, 1919 Alvin York is mustered out of the army and becomes a private citizen.

May 30, 1919 York reaches his beloved family, friends, and future wife, Gracie Williams.

June 7, 1919 Alvin and Gracie are wed by Tennessee Governor Roberts in York's peaceful valley, just outside of

Pall Mall in a field set aside for the occasion.

June 5, 1920 Gracie delivers their first child, Alvin Jr., but the child dies four days later of hydrocephalus.

February 14, 1920 The state of Tennessee deeds a beautiful newly-built home to Alvin and Gracie on the former land of his ancestors, who settled the Wolf Valley.

March 18, 1921 2nd son, Alvin Jr., is born to the Yorks. He is now deceased.

April 20, 1922 Sam K. Cowan publishes Alvin York's life story called, *Sergeant York and His People.*

July 27, 1923 George Edward York is born; alive at the time of this writing.

April 13, 1925 Tennessee State legislation approves the Alvin C. York Agriculture Institute in Jamestown, the Fentress County seat.

September 4, 1925 Woodrow Wilson York is born. He is now deceased.

February 6, 1928 York receives $10,000 advance money for the publishing of his long- sought personal war journal, *Sergeant York: His Own Life Story and War Diary.* This work was accomplished by Australian author, Tom Skeyhill.

1929 Sam Houston, York's 5th son dies of meningitis before his second birthday.

April 14,1930 Andrew Jackson York is born. At the time of this writing, he serves as a park ranger at the Alvin York home in Pall Mall, TN.

April 23,1930 Tom Skeyhill publishes another work called, *Last of the Long Hunters,* a book on the early ancestry of Alvin York and the valley where he lived.

February 25, 1933 Alvin and Gracie celebrate the arrival of their first girl, christened Betsy Ross York. At the time of this writing, she is still living.

September 23, 1935 Mary Alice York is born who now is deceased.

May 7, 1936 York is placed on the Prohibition Party's ticket as vice-president to Dr. D. Colvin. York declines, unwilling to run against President Roosevelt whom he favored.

January 9, 1938 Thomas Jefferson York is born. He dies in the line of duty as deputy sheriff in Pall Mall, TN, on May 7, 1972. At the time of this writing his gracious widow, Margaret, is the hostess of the Alvin York home in Pall Mall, TN.

July 31, 1939 York, Gracie, Pastor Pile,and Pastor R. D. Brown, along with their lawyer, register a charter for the incorporation of Alvin C. York Bible School in Pall Mall, TN. The school was never fully completed.

March 23, 1940 York signs a contract with producer Jesse Lasky and Parmount Pictures for the rights to film the *Sergeant York story.*

November 2, 1940 Gracie York gives birth to a daughter who dies soon after her birth and is left unnamed. This is their last child.

February 26, 1942 Gary Cooper receives the Best Actor of the Year Oscar for role playing Sergeant Alvin York. Upon receiving the award Cooper humbly said, "It wasn't Gary Cooper who won this award; it was Sergeant York. Because to the best of my ability, I tried to be Sergeant York."

May 11, 1943 York files protest with IRS on discrepancies of insufficient income paid for film royalties. This begins an 18-year battle with the IRS.

February 24, 1954 Alvin York suffered a cerebral hemorrhage, leaving him confined to his bed and wheelchair.

March 26, 1961 Ed Sullivan, television host, makes an appeal on behalf of Sergeant York, for the American people to rally around him and help pay his on-going IRS bill. The American people immediately began to send money, and within one month, York's entire bill was paid. Enough money was left to help Gracie and York in their retiring age.

September 2, 1964 Alvin York dies at the age of 76 years old in the Veterans' Hospital in Nashville, Tennessee.

September 27, 1984 Gracie York dies at Park View Hospital in Nashville, Tennessee, at the age of 84.

CHAPTER 1

Boyhood

I was borned in Pall Mall, in Fentress County. Hit is under the mountain; that is to say, in the valley below. Hit is called the Valley of the Three Forks of the Wolf, because Wolf River forks into three branches not far from our home. Hit is in the Cumberland Mountains, in the eastern part of middle Tennessee, not far from the Kentucky line. I was borned in a one-room log cabin with puncheon floors, and the walls made of rough-hewn slabs. These walls was chinked with bark and mud, but jes the same, in the winter time the wind would whistle in through the walls and up through the cracks in the floor. Some of them-there floor cracks were so big we could look and see the chickens and pigs underneath. I was the third in a family of eleven children, eight boys and three girls. Most all of them were big and red-headed; and I was borned and growed up the biggest of them all. There was a whole litter of us and we jes sort of growed up like a lot of little pigs. I don't mean we was allowed to be dirty like pigs. I jes sorter mean that we were most always turned loose out-of-doors on the mountainside, kinder running wild, playing and hunting around. We was sort of brung up by the hair of the head.

We weren't pampered. Mother and Father hadn't any time to pamper us. They was most awful hardworking people. They had to be to bring up eleven children like they did. Father was a blacksmith. His shop was in a cave or rockhouse, as we called it, at the head of the spring on the mountainside, just near our home. He knowed wonderful well how to handle mares and horses and never refused even the meanest of them. Some of the mules was most awful, but my father never backed up on them. I am telling you that shows character. But money was scarce in them times and he never made more than about fifty cents a day. I don't mean to say he averaged that much. He didn't. He was so fond of hunting that he would neglect his blacksmithing and go out over the hills for days to get him some deer or some turkeys. But he wasn't lazy and like the rest of us boys it wasn't natcheral for him to resist the baying of the hounds and the call of the woods. I guess we've got it in the blood. He was a right-smart woodsman. He could follow a trail anywhere, or go out through the wildest country on the darkest nights, and never get lost for a minute. He was the best shot in the mountains. Often I have seed him take the centre out of a target, shot after shot. I have seed him fire a dozen times at a target and put most all of the bullets through the same hole.

We most always had plenty of fresh meat from my father's rifle-gun. But jes the same, we was always poor. Mother used to hire out and work at other places, washing, spinning or weaving, or doing chores. She would earn about twenty-five cents a day.

So we growed up. We had our own log cabin and a little land. We raised chickens and hogs and some corn and we had a couple of cows and a whole heap of fresh air and plenty of room outside, but not much inside the cabin. Eleven children and mother and father take up a most awful lot of room, and that little one-room log cabin was kinder crowded at night, when we were all tucked in; but we was all under one roof, growing up good, strong, and healthy, and loving each other. Jes a mountain family. We children would all lie in bed, tucked in for the night. Mother would sit in front of the big open fire carding, or spinning, or weaving; and Father would sit in the corner in the light of a lantern or a grease lamp and clean and mend his guns; and that's the way we growed up.

We shore were pretty rough scrappers, and among ourselves and with the neighbours' children we used to fight right sharp. Of course, a whole heap of children like that will get up to all sorts of mischief, but Mother jes knowed where the most stinging hickory sticks growed and Father had a mule whip, and they

"Where the road tumbles down to the solid log cabin 'Old Coonrod' Pile had built (2), to the spring and the York home (1). The roadway comes down from the top of 'The Knobs,' a thousand feet above, and it comes over rocks of high and low degree, a jolting, impressive journey for its traveler."

"It was from this home that Alvin went to war, and it was to it he returned."

both knowed how to use them. I guess the reason I growed up so big was that I was such a roughneck and Father had to whip me so much that he sorter kept my hide loose so that I could fill out. When I was sixteen I was nearly six feet tall and weighed one hundred and sixty pounds. Of course, they wanted us to go to school and we was most all anxious to get some larnin'. But we were very poor, and 'most all the other mountain people were poor too, and there was only money enough for the school to keep going about two and a half months each year, and that was in the middle of summer. It was too cold in the wintertime. The roads were bad. There were no bridges over the creeks and we couldn't get across; and we couldn't afford warm clothes neither. And even in the summertime they had to dismiss school for two or three weeks for crops and foddering. I went for about three weeks a year for about five years. I lamed to read and write. I had about a second-grade education. I don't think I could have passed the second grade. The schoolhouse was a little frame one-room building over on the hill. There were about one hundred pupils and only one teacher. We used to sit on benches made out of split logs with two pegs mortised in them. The benches had no backs. They were so high that when I used to sit on them I could scarcely touch the floor with my feet. During the last year we had two or three desks.

I never read no books till I was about twenty years of age. Then I read only one and that was the life of Frank and Jesse James.

I begun to work almost as soon as I could walk. At first I would help Mother around the house, carrying water, getting a little stovewood, and carrying and nursing the other children to keep them from yelling around after Mother while she was trying to get a bite of dinner for us all. I would go out to the field with Father before I was six years old. I would have to chop the weeds out of the corn. Father would be ploughing with the old mule, and I and my brothers would follow after until he was out of sight, and then I we would steal off and play and scrap around; and then when we would get home he would give us some hickory tea, as he called it.

And it didn't take much of it to make a fellow wish there never was no hickory in these-here mountains. Our clothes was very poor. When I first went to school I wore a home-made linsey dress, and I guess I warned it that long it couldn't stay on me no longer nohow, and jes dropped off as if by itself. As I "rowed older and larger Mother would get some clothes from the neighbours, old ones for washings she done for them, to make us boys britches and coats to keep us warm in the winter months. We had clean cotton shirts which we were only allowed to wear on Sunday mornings, but we had no coats. I shore do remember the kind of shoes we wore in the wintertime. Father made them. They was brogan shoes with brass on the toes, and when we would get up in the morning our shoes would be cold and stiff and we would have to warm them around the old log fire before we could put them on. They were most awful hard and stiff and would take the hide off our heels and they slipped up and down when we walked.

When I was sixteen Mother went to the little country store and bought me a pair of dress shoes. I called them Sunday shoes, for I only wore them on Sunday. They were number ten men's shoes. They were the first dress shoes I ever had. I was most awful proud of them. The next Sunday morning Mother and I started to the little church meeting. Of course, I put on the new shoes. I shore felt good in them. I kept looking down at them, and I kinder thought that everybody else was admiring them. Before I got to church it come up a rain and got muddy and the red clay was very tough and pulled off one of the heels. I scraped in the mud, got it, and put it in my front pants pocket. I kept on a-going with one heel on and one off. When I got almost to the church the other heel come off and I got it and put it in my other front pocket. My, what trouble I was with my with first pair of Sunday shoes with both heels off even before I got to church where I could really show them off, and I had no

"The little church which sits by the road with no homes near it is the geographical as well as the religious center of the community—it is the heart of Pall Mall."

coat and my shirt was all wet and muddy too I And there was a girl friend there that I kinder admired. So there I was with my first pair of Sunday shoes and my first time to wear them, and this trouble had to come, and I was slipping all over the road with those number tens with no heels on them, and that shore spoiled the pleasure of the day.

As I growed up I begun to look around for some work, but there wasn't much of it in the little valley. Father took me into the rockhouse, where I helped him to blacksmith. He taught me to handle them there mules and not to back up on them. I got to know horses and mules right smart, and I picked up the blacksmith business. But I most loved getting out with Father to help him shoot. We would hunt the red and gray foxes in the daytime and skunks, possums, and coons after dark. Often we would hunt all day and do the blacksmithing at night. I did a heap of farming too. I worked for Mr. E. J. Williams and others for forty cents a day.

In 1911 when I was 24 years old my dear father takened sick and died of typhoid fever. He was kicked most awful bad by a mule he was trying to shoe. She lashed out and got him. She was the only one that ever out-smarted him. She would not have done it nohow, only he didn't know she was mean. He was most awful sick for some time and I think it led up to his death. That left my mother with a family of eleven small children. Although I was only a young boy, I had to go out and work with the men to help support Mother and the smaller children.

Mother York, the wonderful pioneer mother of America's most distinguished soldier

CHAPTER 2

Gone Hog-Wild

When my father died I sorter went to pieces for a few years. I know I shouldn't have. I ought to have hewed to the line closer than ever, but I didn't. I was at that age, too, when a young man thinks that it's right smart to drink and cuss and fight and tear things up. I sort of felt that was the right-smart way to come into my manhood. And coming into your manhood is like suddenly coming into a lot of riches—you may not appreciate it at first, and sorter squander it.

I begun to drink and gamble jes a little at the start, but it gowed on me. I got in with a crowd of gay fellows and before long I sure was drifting. There was plenty of liquor around. It was very cheap; about sixty-five cents or seventy-five cents a quart. Poker and other gambling games were pretty popular, and smoking and chewing was supposed to be the things. I was a big fellow, strong and hard, too, from black smithing and farming and hunting. I didn't know my own strength. I thought I could whip anybody.

At the beginning we used to have a few drinks of a week-end and sit up nights, gambling our money away; and of course, like most of the others, was always smoking and cussing. I don't think I was mean and bad... I jes played with these things at first, and thee' they got a-hold of me and began to play with my life. I went from bad to worse. I began really to like liquor and gambling, and I was 'most always spoiling for a fight.

There was a bunch of us. There was Everett Delk, Marion Leffew and Marion Delk, who is dead now, and a couple of my brothers. We were a wild crowd; wilder then wild bees when they're swarming. Of a week-end we would go across the Kentucky line and get drunk and look for trouble, and we shore enough found it.

Back in the days before the World War the Kentucky-Tennessee state line was a tough place. There were drinking shacks, "blind tigers" we used to call them, most every few miles. I am a-telling you Sodom and Gomorrah might have been bigger places, but they weren't any worse. Killings were a-plenty. They used to say that they used to shoot fellows jes to see them kick. Knife fights and shooting were common, gambling and drinking were commoner, and lots of careless girls jes used to sorter drift in. It shore was tough. They used to build these wooden shacks right on the line, half in one state and half in the other. If you come from Tennessee and wanted to buy liquor and booze you went across to the Kentucky pare of the building. If you come from Kentucky you crossed over to the Tennessee side. That was to befoul the law and sorter protect yourselves and the people who were running the places. We used to go over there 'most every week-end and after we was filled up with liquor we would go back in the trees and gamble and roam around, or go dancing and looking for trouble.

The liquor we used to drink in those days was most often jes plain Tennessee or Kentucky moonshine. That's powerful liquor. There was plenty of it; and we jes natcherly knowed how to put it away. We would often drink over a quart each a night, and two or three quarts each over a week-end. That's a lot of liquor. We used to think it right smart to drink each other down.

I ricollect oncet a bunch of us got us each a quart of moonshine whiskey and a quart of apple brandy, and we had a sorter drinking bout. We would drink so long as we could stand up, but when we fell over or passed out we would what you might call disqualify.

The one who drunk the most and stayed on his feet the longest got all of the liquor that was left. We bought the liquor at Ball Rock, which is right on the line, and then we come back around Caney Creek and went to it.

There were six of us and we shore put away a lot of that-there liquor. My brothers Henry and Albert didn't last long.

They each put away about three quarters of that apple brandy, and that was the end of them. Everett Delk and me guzzled up a quart each, and then I am a-telling you we were rarin' to go. We started out for Jim Crabtree's house. There was some right-smart girls there; fine girls and good looking too. And though we could hardly stand nohow, we kinder thought we would like to have a little dance with them. We crossed over through a sage field and drunk some more liquor. I guess that old field was pretty flat country, but it seems most awful hilly to me. I knowed I was a-going; and sure enough, another drink and I was flat on my back; but Everett kept a-going and a-drinking.

He went to the house and swallowed a most awful lot of buttermilk, which sorter brought him around. He then went back around the field and collected up all the liquor that was left and took it back to the house and hid it upstairs. Then he kinder kicked and shook us awake. We was scattered here and yonder, jes wherever we give up. We began to come to and go into the house all the way from seven o'clock till midnight. Next morning we didn't none of us know what we had done with our whiskey. We thought we drunk it all. We felt like it, too. But Everett went upstairs and got it and we went to it again. That was the kind of drinking we used to do.

Another time we had to light out from home and go over near the state line and hide us from the grand jury which was after us. They wanted us for liquoring up and fighting and carrying weapons. They didn't have any specific charges against us. They jes wanted to get us before them and question us. And we jes knowed if they ever got us before them and got to questioning us we shore would give each other away and be indicted. So we went over there near the line and jes drinked and gambled and played around until it kinder blew over.

Once they got me for being mixed up in carrying and selling a weapon. I used to always tote a gun around with me and a knife, too. I went before the jury and got out of it right smart. I pleaded my own case and proved to them that it was not my gun, that I was jes delivering it for somebody else. But hit shore was close and they come near getting me. Another time I was riding home on a mule, drunk as a saloon fly, and sorter wanting to shoot things up. It was in the very early morning. I saw some turkey gobblers sitting on the fence and up in a tree. I had a pistol with me. I jes couldn't resist seeing if my nerve was all right. I jes fired six shots from a long way off, and the air was full of feathers, and there was six dead turkeys stretched out on the ground. Now that was one time that my marksmanship got me in bad. I was brung up before the court, but was able to buy out of it. Turkeys are pretty valuable around our way, especially when it's near Thanksgiving, and it's a pretty serious offence to muss them up.

Once Everett and I were full of booze and riding home on the same mule, both of us, one behind the other. How we done it I don't know; neither of us could sit up straight. But we done it. In the darkness we saw something white sorter floating on Caney Creek. Everett thought it was a white pillow, and I didn't know what it was. We were that full that we couldn't see straight. I got out the old gun again and let fly and we heard an awful squawking and fluttering about in the water, and whatever it was begun to float off. Everett went down to investigate. He said there was feathers and blood all over the water. Then we knowed I had killed a tame goose. I had shot it plumb through the breast. So we thought we had better get out while the going was good, and we did. It was Mr. Moody's goose, and I guess he doesn't know to this day who it was that bumped it off.

Not having no money never bothered us much. We could make it all right at shooting matches. I sure could bust a turkey's head at 'most any distance and cut the center out of a target and win the prize money most any time. I used to do the shooting and Everett would do the betting and then when we won we would buy us some more liquor.

I am a-telling you I kept going from bad to worse, drinking

more and more, and gambling whenever I had the chance or the money, and fighting a whole heap. I was never oncet whipped or knocked off my feet. I jes kinder thought I could whip the world and more than oncet I set out to do it.

I was in a couple of shooting frays too. You see the only book I had read was the life of Frank and Jesse James. It made a big impression on me. I used to practice and practice to shoot like them James boys. I used to get on my mule and gallop around and shoot from either hand and pump bullet after bullet in the same hole. I used to even throw the pistol from hand, to hand and shoot jes as accurate. I could take that old pistol and knock off a lizard's or a squirrel's head from that far off that you could scarcely see it. So you see I was kinder handy when it come to hitting the mark. I never did kill nobody. I never did really fire at anybody; that is, not to hit them. I often shot a few bullets in their direction to frighten them off. Once we hired to a fellow to take some cattle from Wolf River to Chanute. We got four dollars for that. . So we took it to Lick Creek and bought us that much whiskey. That was enough to make us pretty full. We was riding along on our mules and we met up with Will Huff, and we decided to have some fun with him. I got out my little pearl-handle revolver and began to shoot at the ground underneath his mule's belly. That sorter knocked the rocks loose and they flew up and hit the mule and it got to bucking and thronged Will off. He was not hurt, but he was most awful mad.

Then we got to firing under my mule and it bucked me off. I was that wobbly I couldn't sit straight and I jes sorter fell off, and I lay where I fell, too. Everett got him a paling off'n the fence and proceeded to bring me around by slapping me with that old wooden paling. I come to and, thinking somebody was after me, I jumped on the old mule and galloped like an express train through the trees. I guess an express train couldn't have catched me. I lost my hat, but I kept on a-going, shooting and hollering and cussing as I rode. After a few miles I fell off and went to sleep again. I got into a knife fight, too, with one of the boys in our valley. It was on a Sunday morning after church and that made it worse. We were both full of moonshine and that started it. We sure would have cut each other up, but some of the other boys got between us and separated us. It was over a girl. I am a-telling you that wine and women make a bad mix-up.

Then there was a fellow named Maxey. We had a most awful argument down at a stave mill, and he said next time we met he was going to get me. A few days later I decided to wait for him on the road and run him off. So when he come along I fired a few shots near his feet, and knocked up the dust, and told him to go; and he done went, too. I never seed him again.

I ain't a-boasting of these days. I am kinder ashamed of them now. They was most awful bad. They couldn't have been worser without me killing or hurting somebody; but I never did that. I did enough just the same. I drunk liquor whenever I could get it. I was drunk most every week-end. I gambled away most of my hard-earned money. I was always chewing and cussing. I was always wanting to whip somebody.

I am a-saying again that old Kentucky line was a tough place, and the boys around there was tough too, tougher than hickory; and I was one of them. I was always in trouble, or looking for trouble, and it looked as if sooner or later I would get it and get it right smart. I tell you I was hog-wild.

CHAPTER 3

Rough Livin'

I ain't had much of the larnin' that comes out of books. I'm a-trying to overcome that, but it ain't easy. If ever you let life get the jump on you, you have to keep hiking to catch up with it again, and I never knowed the truth of this like I do now. It ain't my fault. It ain't nobody's fault. It jes happened. We were most all poor people in the mountains when I was a boy. We hadn't neither the time nor the money to get much larnin'. The roads were bad. There were creeks to cross. So I "rowed up uneducated. And I never will stop regretting it. Only the boy who is uneducated can understand what an awful thing ignorance is. And when he is suddenly pushed out into the world and has to live with educated people and has to hear them discussing things he can't understand, he then sorter realizes what he has missed. And I'm a-telling you he suffers a lot.

When I joined the army I immediately knowed what a terrible handicap my lack of schooling was. When I went over to Paris and visited all sorts of places and seed things I didn't know nothing about nohow, I jes wished I could have had my early life over again. I jes knowed I would have got some larnin' somewhere. Then when I come back home again and found so many people knowed and wanted to meet me, I kinder felt all mussed up about it. But until I begun this book I never fully understood how necessary an education is and how little chance you have to get anywhere without it. When I sit down to write I know what I want to say, but I don't always know jes how to put it down on paper. I jes don't know how to get it out of me and put it in words. I ain't had the training. Hit's no use kicking about it. I suppose I have to do the best I can. I can't do no more. All the same, I do wish I could have had the advantages of good schools and books and teachers.

I have promised myself that I am going to get these things for my children; and for a heap of other children too. I'm a-dedicating my life to building schools in the mountains. If it is necessary I'm going to build good roads and bridges and provide transportation so that the children can get to these schools too. If they can't afford it nohow, I'm a-going to give them a chance to work their way through.

Mountain people are not great readers. I don't mean the people in the towns and more settled communities in the mountain country, I mean we-tins right in the mountains. It is hard to get books and there ain't no libraries. But we're most all good storytellers. And we repeat our stories over and over again until they become sort of household news. Whenever you get two mountaineers together you 'most always get a story. Around the old blacksmith shop, at the store, or at the shooting matches you are most certain to hear a whole mess of them; and when we visit each other and sit around the old open fireplaces on long winter nights we tell a right-smart lot of them. Hunting and shooting stories are the most popular.

And the best of them are remembered and handed down from father to children, jes like the muzzle-loading guns and the old dresses. We never seem to tire of hearing about old Davy Crockett's bear hunts and Daniel Boone's fights with the Indians. And we have all kinds of stories of Andrew Jackson and Sam Houston. They used to get around these parts. There's a whole heap of Crocketts living in Jimtown to this day. These old-timers must have been right-smart men. We don't find the like of them around nowadays. But times have changed. Maybe we don't live the sort of lives which make great men.

Since I was knee high to a duck I've heard tell of these men. I guess what outsiders call history is jes plain story-telling with us.

So you see we mountaineers, without having read many books or studying the subject are tol'ably well informed of what has done been in these parts since the time of the first settlers. The records have been repeated in story form and handed down year after year until it comes to us.

These-here mountains of old Tennessee, North Carolina, and Kentucky were once the hunting and fighting grounds of the Cherokees and Creeks. They was jes about the fightinest Indians that ever put on the war paint. I guess the panthers and wild cats must have studied their methods. Them-there Indians must have been kinder fond of these-here parts. The bears and buffaloes must have attracted them. There sure must have been a mess of them around here. It was nothing for the early settlers to shoot a hundred bear in a single season. They say that Davy Crockett shot ten in one day. I'm a-telling you that's a lot of bear.

Daniel Boone once saw so many buffaloes grazing in the valleys of these-here Cumberland mountains that he shouted, "I am richer than the man mentioned in the Scripture, who owned the cattle of a thousand hills; I own the wild beasts of more than a thousand valleys." And there must have been a lot of deer on the hoof. Some of the old settlers in the mountains still have the fringed deerskin shirts and moccasins of their pioneer ancestors. And there were coon, fox, and panther and all sorts of other varmints. There still are.

But the white settlers come in and started things. The first to come were the fighting Scotch-Irish. They come from the borders of Scotland and from the north of Ireland. They were followed by the Cavaliers from the hills of Scotland and by the Covenanters from England, the Huguenots from France, and a number of Germans. But the Scotch-Irish outnumbered all the others. They were the first. They stayed right on and these mountains are full of their descendants to-day. These old settlers were the most independent, God-fearing and God-loving people in the world. They left the other side rather than bow down to kings and dictators and accept political and religious beliefs they didn't believe in nohow. So they come over here where they hoped to be able to govern themselves and worship

God according to the dictates of their own conscience. They followed the Quakers over into Pennsylvania and then hiked down the Shenandoah Valley to the mountains of North Carolina, and from there they fought their way through the Smokies over into the Cumberlands and Kentucky. That's how Daniel Boone travelled.

He was a kind of trail blazer. Wherever he led others followed; that is, if they got past the Indians. They fought it out all over this country. It was tough fighting from the start to the finish. They tomahawked and shot and scalped each other until nigh every inch of these mountains and valleys was stained with human blood. "The Dark and Bloody Ground" begins only a few miles from where I live. There was no stopping them-there early pioneers. They gave the Indians the best they had. It was enough. When they started anything they stuck it out until it was done finished. They believed the only good Indian was a dead one; so they proceeded to make them all good. And they did a right-smart job of it. There are not many redskins left today; and them that are live by themselves on Government reservations. The trouble was there wasn't room enough for both to live in this-here country. What happened is what always happens, when two people fight the strongest won. And the new settlers happened to be the strongest. That's the way of nature.

They were the fightinest men. They were always at it. If it was not the Indians, it was the English or French or Spanish. The Tennessee Sharpshooters were in the thick of it at King's Mountain. They went up the slopes and sharpshooted Ferguson and his Red Coats until there was nigh on none of them left. That-there Ferguson was a tol'able hard-fighting man himself, and he and his troops were great favourites with Cornwallis. And our mountain men shot them all to pieces. That was one of the turning battles in the Revolutionary War. The Tennessee Sharpshooters were Andrew Jackson's favourite troops. Their old long-barrelled muzzle-loaders did a whole heap to whip the English at New Orleans.

They were up against it there too. They were fighting the pick of Wellington's veterans, the ones who helped to bust Napoleon. And the mountaineers out-fought and out-shot them. They were well in it, too, at Pensacola and later on in Mexico. My grandfather, Uriah York, was in the Mexican War and took part in the storming of the heights of Chapultepec. Them-there old pioneers was always fighting. Whenever their liberty was threatened they went right at it. And once when they figured their own Government was not doing the right thing by them they up and founded the free and independent State of Franklin, which was in eastern Tennessee. If you step on a rattler he will strike, and if you step on a Scotch Irishman or a Highlander he will jes natcherly hit back until somebody gets hurt.

The descendants of them-there old pioneers are the mountaineers of to-day. We haven't changed so very much. Of course, we don't wear deerskin shirts and moccasins and coonskin caps. We get on tol'ably well now in overalls and jeans. The old muzzle-loaders are givin' way to the modern high-powered rifle and shotgun—but jes the same there are a right-smart lot of hog rifles, as we hunters call them, in the mountains even to-day. Most all of us know how to load them, with cap and ball; and up to one hundred yards prefer them to any other rifle in the world. The modern home is drivin' out the little old log cabin with the rough-hewn logs and puncheon floors, but they ain't all gone. You see them here and there through the mountains. My brother George still lives in the one in which we "rowed up."

Even if our clothes and guns and homes are changing, we still sort of hang on to the old pioneer's love of political and religious liberty. We haven't much use for rituals and prayer books. Our God is still the God of our ancestors—the God of the Old Testament. We still believe in His word as it has been revealed to us in the old Bible. In politics too we still hang on to the old ideals of liberty and states' rights. In our family life too we are much the same. Blood is still pretty thick around these-here parts, and we still stick together much like the clans of our ancestors.

The mountains have sorter hemmed us in along with our own beliefs and ways of living. We kinder live an Eighteenth Century life, in the middle of the Twentieth Century. You can kinder trace our pedigree in the names of the towns all through the mountains. There is Pall Mall, where I live; and Jamestown, the county site; and Livingston, close by; and Cookeville, and Crossville, and Rugby. Them's good old Anglo-Saxon names. And to kinder balance things, there is Possum Trot, Coon Gap, Wolf Valley, Wolf River, and Burrville. There's the pioneer side of us. And jes like the towns which are a mixture of old Anglo-Saxon and the spirit of the frontier days, so we-tins are a mixture of old Anglo-Saxon stock, kinder seasoned and hardened in the roughness of this-here new continent of ours.

So we people in the mountains claim that while we are good Americans, the sons and daughters of early pioneers, we are also the old Anglo-Saxon type and among the purest in America. We still sing many of the old border ballads and speak a heap of old English words, like "ain't," "we-uns," "you-uns," and "afeared." We are big and rangy and raw-boned. And there are 'most any number of red-headed people all around. We have a saying that you may see a red-headed man in the penitentiary, but you will never see one in an insane asylum.

CHAPTER 4

Guns A-Plenty

Most all of the mountain people have jes natcherly growed up with rifles. From the cradle they are sorter used to the smell of powder and the presence of the old muzzle-loader, powder horn, and doeskin shot pouch hanging in a corner of the cabin. The mountaineer's arm has a sort of natural crook for an old rifle-gun.

The rifle played a big part in the conquering and developing of this-here mountain country. I ain't got much poetry in me, but any I have I sorter spill out on rifles and shooting and hunting. I am sorter used to these things. I understand them. I know how to make the most of them.

I am telling you I would much sooner take up my muzzle-loader than a pen or pencil, and I am much more useful with it, too. The early pioneers not only knowed how to use their rifles, but they knowed how to make them. The long-barrel, muzzle-loading type of rifle made in the mountains of North Carolina, Tennessee, and Kentucky was the best and most accurate shooting gun in the world, and up to one hundred yards it still is. At the two last turkey-shooting matches held in our valley, seven out of ten of the turkeys had their heads busted with the muzzle-loaders and only three with modern rifles. The distance was 'most always sixty yards, but the old muzzle-loaders also brought down turkeys at one hundred fifty yards, although they are not so good as the modern rifle at that distance.

Before the American pioneers made and sort of perfected these-here muzzle-loaders there was really no accurate rifle-guns in the world. The old flintlocks, muskets, and blunderbusses which they used over therein Europe were not much account nohow. They were never sure of hittin' the mark. They were never even sure of goin' off, and even when they did they made a noise like a cannon. They often done more damage to the shooter than to the one he was shootin' at. Most often the powder flared back into the eyes of whoever was squintin' down the barrel. Them-there guns might have been all right over there on the other side where a miss didn't matter so much and there was plenty of time to reload and the more noise the better, but they never would have got nothin' nohow over here. The hunters who come into the American wilderness fightin' Indians and shootin' game for food jes couldn't afford to miss. They had to have a rifle-gun that they knowed would shoot straight; that would shoot 'most every time they fired it; that they could reload pretty quick, and that wouldn't make too much noise for the Indians to hear. They couldn't get these guns nowhere. There weren't any. So they begun to make them themselves. And they made the first accurate, dependable guns in the world. I guess the first real good guns that come down here to the mountains were the Decherds in Pennsylvania, but soon the mountaineers begun to get busy and made their own.

Most all around this-here mountain country there was blacksmiths and gunsmiths in them-there days who learned how to make rifles that jes knowed how to shoot straight. To this day there are men who can make them. And if you roam around for a while you can still see the ruins of the crude old blast furnaces they used. I spent a heap of my time as a boy black smithing with my father. I never made any guns but I often doctored sick ones. I know the heap of trouble and care you have to take when you are fooling around with guns. And yet, these old Southern gunsmiths with crude forges and cruder home-made equipment turned out guns that served the purpose and revere in their time the best guns in the world and are even now thought a heap of by our mountain marksmen. These old mountain guns were made from ore dug out of these-here mountains. Even the barrels were bored or welded and then rifled on the ground. The trigger, trigger guard, firing pan, flint chops, sights, and all the other fittings were also made right in the mountains and the stock was generally carved out of “rained and seasoned woods, such as bird’s-eye maple, or curly cherry, or black walnut.

Some of the best known of these old mountain guns were the Gibsons, Beans, or Duncans. Later on, of course, the barrels and the locks were bought outside and shipped in; and to-day nearly all the other parts are bought and assembled. But jes the same there are a heap of them old pioneer guns around, and there arc a few mountain gunsmiths still left who can turn them out almost as good as ever. We don’t use the flintlocks to-day. Hit is too hard to keep them dry. Out in the woods we always had to keep them covered with a sort of sleeve which we slip over the barrel. This sleeve was generally made from the skin of a steer or a deer’s leg. Armed with these old mountain guns, not more than nine hundred mountain sharpshooters whipped and shot to pieces Ferguson and his twenty-six hundred trained men at King’s Mountain. And it was these same old guns which made it possible for the six thousand men under Andrew Jackson down there at New Orleans to stop ten thousand British soldiers who once fought under Wellington and mussed up Napoleon.

Allowing for the times and the conditions and the purposes for which they were used, them-there native made guns were the best rifle-guns that was ever made. I myself have used the Army service rifles and most of the modern high-powered rifles, but when I go hunting or take part in the shooting matches up to one hundred or even up to one hundred and fifty yards I much prefer my old muzzle-loading rifle-gun to any other in the world, and that’s what I think of it.

They are very cheap to keep up. Loading ain’t no bother if you know how. First of all, you stand the old gun upright with the butt resting on the ground. Then you pour the powder out of a powder horn, made from the horn of a buck or a steer, into the charger, which is generally carved out of the tip of a buck’s horn. The amount of powder you use, of course, depends on the distance you expect to shoot. Natcherly, a long shot takes a bigger charge of powder than a short shot. You pour the powder out of the charger down the muzzle of the gun. Many shooters are so expert that they can measure off the powder in the hollow of their hands and empty it into the muzzle, scarcely losing a grain. Then the patch is placed over the end of the muzzle. This-here patch is generally a piece of blue denim or bed ticking and it is best when it is greased or tallowed. The ball is then taken out of the shot pouch, which is made of soft doeskin and placed on top of the patch and pressed with the thumb into the barrel. Then the ends of the patch are trimmed off and the bullet and the patch are rammed hard down against the powder. The ramrod is generally a straight piece of hickory whittled into shape. A couple of whangs with this-here ramrod packs the ball into place. The patch lies on top of the powder and sorter packs the ball tight in the barrel so that the explosion can't escape. Last of all, the little percussion cap is put in place. Then the gun is ready for firing. All this takes jes a short time. Many of the old-timers can reload these old guns on the run.

Of course, if you're a hunter you have got to know all about guns and how to handle them. Guns are like hounds, they have a lot of this-here temperament, and you have got to kinder get acquainted with them. Sometimes you have got to kinder kid them. A gun will shoot a certain way one day and altogether different the next day. You have got to know whether they shoot fine or full, or to the left or to the right; how the wind affects them, and the sunlight and the clouds; even how they shoot on damp days and dry days. I have a whole collection of them at home. I have an automatic shotgun and a twenty-five-twenty rifle and that old muzzle-loader of my father's. It's the cap-and-ball type. My father done used it in the shooting matches, and that's what I use it for now. It's a sure gun for that sort of work. It jes don't know how to miss nohow. And I have a forty-five pistol. I sure would like to have the one I used in the fight with the machine guns in the Argonne. I tried to get it. The War

Department searched through about fifty thousand pistols for it, but I guess somebody got a-hold of it and knowed it was a good one and decided to keep it.

I kinder think that the reason why the mountaineers are among the best shots in the world is because they have "rowed up with rifles. They know all about them. They know how to take them to pieces and put them together again. They know how to doctor them when they're sick, and many of them even know how to make them. I am a-telling you that's understanding a gun. Then they are always using them out in the woods shooting at all sorts of game. Of course, that's great practice. Then 'most all of them live pretty healthy outdoor lives and go in for regular hours, natcheral food, and the right amount of sleep. So their sight and their nerves are 'most always good.

And then there's the shooting matches which are always very popular in the mountains. Busting a turkey's head and cutting the centre of targets makes for expert marksmanship. A right-smart heap of the men who went to King's Mountain and whipped Ferguson went right from one of these-here shooting matches. They were a-having a big time of it. They were shooting for beeves and turkeys at a big match at Gilbertown, N. C., when they received word from Ferguson, telling them if they didn't lay down their arms and return to their rightful allegiance he would come over them-there hills and smash their settlements and hang their leaders. They was jes about the best shooters in the mountains and they went straight from that shooting match and connected with the backwater men and went up King's Mountain and showed Ferguson how American mountaineers, armed with American muzzle-loading rifle-guns, can shoot.

CHAPTER 5

Turkeys Don't Live Long

Most every Saturday of late we have been holding these old-fashioned shooting matches on a hillside on my farm here in Pall Mall. Last Saturday we had one. We usually shoot for turkeys and end up the day with a beeve. We tie the turkeys behind logs with only their heads showing and shoot offhand; that is, standing up from a mark sixty yards away. We draw for positions and then take our turn shooting. We never know when the turkey is going to put his head above the log, or how long he is going to keep it there, or whether he is going to bob or weave just as you have drawn a fine bead on him. He pleases himself about that, and I am a-telling you a turkey gobbler tied behind a log is sometimes the contrariness bird I ever knowed. He jes seems to know the right moment to duck.

We generally pay ten cents a shot and we get the turkey when we bust its head. Sometimes we do that right smart and the owner of the turkey don't get much out of it. Other times, when the wind and the light are agin us, he will collect a heap of dimes before anybody busts the turkey.

My father was p'int-blank certain death on turkeys' heads. He jes didn't know how to miss them. He really was a most wonderful shot. Often they ruled him down; that is, they made him shoot near the last, and sometimes they would never let him shoot nohow They made him act as judge. I recollect a hill-billy from one of the back creeks brought in oncet two big turkey gobblers. He tried to raise a heap of money on them by laying down unfair conditions, but the mountaineers are pretty smart. They jes wouldn't shoot. He brought the price down to a nickel a shot. Still they wouldn't shoot. He had ruled my father out but at last he let him in to sort of start things; and he sure enough busted that old turkey's head the first shot. The same sort of thing happened over the second turkey, and my father had a pretty good day of it two—big turkey gobblers for ten cents. It is even better sport to shoot at the turkey at one hundred and fifty yards. We tie them to a stake out in the open and from a standing position have to hit them above the knee and below the gills. That's shooting too.

But the big event of these-here shooting matches is the beeve. "Beeve" is jes plain mountain talk for beef, and I guess 'most all over the world a beef means a steer. The beef is driven alive to the shooting ground. Its value is fixed by the owner, and then shots are sold at so much each until the price is made up. If the beef is worth fifty dollars generally fifty shots are sold at one dollar each. The owner takes the money. Each shooter can buy as many shots as he likes, but he has to pay for each shot. The first and second prizes are the hind quarters; the second and third the fore quarters; and the fifth the hide and tallow. That is generally how they are divided up.

The mark to shoot at is the dead centre of a crisscross cut with a sharp knife on a board. Each shooter generally prepares his own board, and he prepares it according to his own liking. Some shooters blacken their boards over a fire of grass and twigs, and then put a little square of white paper either below or above the centre of the criss-cross according to the way they like to draw the bead. Others most like a plain white board with a black mark either under or above the centre of the criss-cross. The shooting is generally so expert that you 'most always have to cut the centre; that is, at least touch it with the bullet, if you hope to even get a smell of the meat; and if you hope to win one of the first choices, ho ! ho ! you generally have to take the centre out, bust it right out; and that's got to be a most powerful true shot. After each man shoots, his board is initialled and held by the judge until the prizes are settled. Often the shots are so close that the bullet has to be cut in half and placed in the hole and a compass used to determine which is the closest shot. My father 'most always was a judge and used to use the compass, and now that he is no more, my brother Sam generally does it.

At the last shooting match we had a right-smart crowd of mountain sharpshooters turn out. They come in from all over the mountains. They come in afoot, on horseback, in wagons, and in automobiles. They come in from away back in the canebreaks, from up the creeks, off the farms, and from the towns around. They come in their blue jeans and overalls and all sorts of other shooting and business clothes. They carried their old muzzle-loaders crooked under their arms and their powder horns and pouches slung over their shoulders. There must have been nearly a hundred of them and they were 'most all of the best shots around this-here part of Tennessee.

John Conatzer, a real hill-billy from back in the mountains, come in and declared he was a-gong to eat turkey that night. He come in right off his little farm. He was dressed in his old overalls, with big patches on the knees and the elbows worn through. He had on an old slouch hat that hadn't any shape nohow. He had almost as much stubble on his chin as a wheat field after the mowing machine has been over it. He wore hobnail shoes and they shore give him a mean grip on the ground. John is jes one of the meanest men in all the mountains when it comes to drawing a fine bead under the centre of a target, or busting a turkey's head at 'most any distance. Winning the first prize is a sort of habit with him. He lives right up on top of a mountain, and he says it's that steep there he has to wear hobnails in the seat of his britches.

John Souders, one of the best shots in all this part of Tennessee, was on the ground early. He said he kinder felt it was his day and them-there turkeys was shore going home with him. I jes can't write well enough to describe his get-up, but I'm a-telling you it was even more artistic than John Conatzer's. Them there two mountaineers seem to be rivals in everything, even in clothes, and they 'moss always take meat home with them. John Souders comes from up one of the back creeks. Away in. He brought his old Decherd with him; the same sorter gun they used at King's Mountain. It stands over six feet and weighs twenty pounds. You can still see the hammer marks on the barrel. It sure is an old-timer.

Ike Hatfield was there, too. He is a descendant of the bushwhackers who raised Cain around these parts in the Civil War, and he is also a relation of the Hatfields who kinder set the fashion for feuds over across the line in Kentucky. Compared with Ike's eyesight, an eagle can't see nothing nohow. He said he was all p'int-blank fired up to bust them old gobblers' heads and to put his bullet inside of anybody else's.

Sheriff Livingston come in with a big crowd from Jimtown. He is well over sixty years of age, but there ain't nothing the matter with his sight or with his nerves neither. That-there old sheriff has raided more moonshiners than has 'most anybody else in these mountains. He's shot bigger game than turkeys, too. He has more'n once killed his man. Whenever he squints down the barrel of a gun, he is jes going to hit plumb in the centre.

Several of my brothers was there Sam, toting my father's old muzzle-loader, which is jes about the favourite gun around here; and Joe, who runs the store at Wolf River; and George, who is jes the shootinest fool when it comes to matches; and Henry and Jim and Albert. They was all there. And they was all most awful keen on carrying off some of them-there prizes. And I am a-telling you I was there and I jes knowed I was a-going to have a turkey dinner that night. I was yes in the right mood for it.

It was a most awful bad day for shooting. The wind was a-blowing and there was a bright sunshine and a blue sky with jes a few thin white clouds kinder driftin' over. I was well down in the draw, so I jes set down and took it easy and kept my nerve steady. I felt plumb shore that I was going to get one of them there turkeys. That-there first gobbler was jes the boldest bird that I ever seed. He jes stuck that-there red head of his up over the log and kinder looked lazily around as though admiring the landscape. The bullets of the first shooters pelted the log under him, knocked the dust out of his gills, or went whizzing past not a hair's breadth away, but not one of them drew blood. He shore seemed to have a charmed life. Every now and then he put his old head down to kinder rest or gobble up something from the ground, and then he kinder become interested agin and bobbed up to see what it was all about.

When John Souders stepped up to shoot, with that old Decherd of hisn I was even more interested than the turkey. He shore must have wanted that turkey most awful bad. He took a long time sighting, drew a fine bead jes above the turkey's gills and then missed. His bullet whanged right past that old gobbler's head and cut up a streak of dust a few yards behind. I'm a-tellin' you that-there old gobbler blinked. That tickled John Conatzer. He said that he knowed that the Lord Almighty was protecting that turkey from harm until his turn come. He took even a longer time than Souder. He jes stood there straight and still with his old muzzle-loader painting what looked like point-blank death at the gobbler. He stood there that long that it seemed that he would never fire nohow. We all sort of got tired holding our breath. Some of the other shooters tried to kid him, but they might jes as well have tried to kid a coon down the tree when the hound dogs are barking underneath. But in spite of everything he missed too, but only by an eyelash. That old turkey was most awful close to being cold meat when John's ball whizzed past.

By this time we was all gifting fired up. Two of the best shots in the valley had fired and missed, and we shore made life miserable for them. It was even more miserable for them than for the turkey. That old gobbler didn't seem to care nohow. He still kept his old red head up, sorter challengin' like. Then young Oliver Delk, who lives back up one of the creeks, toed the mark. He looked pretty young and didn't stand much higher'n the muzzle-loader itself. We wasn't paying much attention to him and the turkey wasn't either. We all kinder counted him

"Up the mountainside above the York spring, a space was cleared for shooting matches, where the prizes were beeves and turkeys, and where the men shot so accurately that the slender crossing of two knife-blade marks was the bull's-eye of the target."

A TYPICAL CREEK-BED ROAD IN THE MOUNTAINS

"And there were only mountain trails and old dirt roads, that were no good nohow, and creek beds here before."

TURKEY-SHOOTING

"We tie the turkeys behind logs with only their heads showing and shoot off-hand; that is, from a standing position, sixty yards away. We pay ten cents a shot and get the turkey if we bust its head.

out as only a tolerable shot. He fired and that-there old turkey ducked, but he come up again right smart, bold as ever. Ike Hatfield was so surprised he swallowed his plug of home-twist and nearly had convulsions. Oliver had scratched it across the head. The skin was jes broken so he claimed it. The rules are that if you draw blood it is your turkey. So young Oliver, as proud as Solomon in all his glory, takened his turkey and another was placed behind the log.

My brother Sam was next to shoot. He complained that he had some dirt in his eye and that he couldn't draw a fine bead nohow. Jes the same he shot so close that I bet that new gobbler held his breath as Sam's bullet went past.

I was feeling pretty good when it come my turn. I told them hill-billies around to watch me right close and they would see what real shooting was. I looked that old gobbler right in the eye and he seemed to me to be looking right back at me and sorter challenged me to put his head down. I drew a pretty fine bead and allowed jes the least little bit for the wind. Then I recollected the sun was shining from the right. I allowed for that too. Then to make real sure I damped the foresight.

I sighted carefully. Then I lowered the rifle and told the boys that I could only have nicked him that time and I wanted to do better'n that. I sighted again and I figured on drilling him right through the head. I could already see that turkey on the table at home for supper. I drew even a finer bead and pressed the trigger, but that-there old gobbler didn't go down. He hadn't any sense nohow. A streak of dust spurted up just behind his head, and I shore enough had missed, ho! ho! My brother George suggested that maybe the bullet had bounced off of the gobbler's head, and John Conatzer 'lowed that I was gittin' old and shaky anyhow.

The next half-dozen shots also missed. That-there sunshine and them-there little white clouds shore made it bad for good shooting.

Mr. H. C. Cravens, who keeps a store in Jimtown, got the

next turkey. He busted it right through the head and it never did know what hit it, unless it thought it was struck by a bolt of lightning.

And, after some more missing, Allen Brooks got the third. It was a plumb good shot, too. After that we lengthened the distance. We tethered the next gobbler to a stake, away under the hill, one hundred and fifty yards away. He shore looked pretty, too, strutting around on the end of the string, with his feathers kinder glistening in the sunlight, and his big red head held proudly up, jes like a peacock's. But he didn't stay up long. My brother George, who is the most awfulest man on long-distance turkey shooting, come up with that-there old muzzle-loading gun of my father's. Some of the boys 'lowed that a hundred and fifty yards was too far for that-there old hog rifle. But George stood up there and hit that turkey that hard it must have thought the hill had fallen on it. It went right up in the air and then come down and spread out all over the ground, stone dead. George had shot it right through the breast with a hog rifle at a hundred and fifty yards.

The turkeys were now going pretty fast. The boys were getting their eyes in and were doing most wonderful things with their rifles. The next turkey we tethered somehow or other managed to get loose jes as one of the boys was taking aim. We all laughed and suggested that he ought to shoot it on the run, but he put down his rifle, spit out a plug of tobacco, and remarked that hit was hard enough to hit them there fool birds when they were still and they was harder to hit than bats when they was moving.

So some of the boys lit out and chased that old turkey through the woods, and run it up against a fence and brought it back to its rightful place, where it spent the next few minutes kinder contentedly picking insects off'n the ground. Some other shooters fired and missed. Their bullets tore up the dirt around the turkey, but he was busy hunting his dinner and didn't mind nohow.

My turn come agin after a while and I was all fired to make up for missing that first shot. I jes couldn't figure on missing this time no way and nohow. I squinted down the barrel of the old muzzle loader and I could see that turkey jes sorter on the end of it. I drew a fine bead agin, allowed for windage and distances, and was jes going to pull the trigger when one of them-there hogs of mine that had been feeding on acorns somewhere in the woods, cantered right across my field of fire.

That kinder tickled the crowd. If it had been a razorback I would have let fly jes the same, but it was one of my prize Poland Chinas, and though I wanted that old turkey most awful bad, I sorter didn't want to ruin the future prospects of that-there hog of mine. I kinder figured I could have cut a couple of his bristles and got the turkey the same, but it ain't natural for a farmer to take chances with hogs, so I waited until he had wandered on a piece, and then I took aim agin and whanged a bullet right at that-there old gobbler. I guess I must have had one eye on the Poland China because I shore missed that turkey by several feet. I didn't even scare it. The bullet kicked up the dust somewhere between the turkey and the hog. So you see, that time I might have been a bad turkey shooter, but I was a most awful careful hog farmer.

The boys shot four turkeys in the next seven shots. That's shootin', I'm a-tellin' you. We kept the last one, a great big gobbler, the best of them all, for the last shootin' of the day.

Then we made up the beeve. But this time the beeve was a hog a two hundred forty pounder. He was valued at twenty-four dollars and we paid fifty cents a shot until the amount was made up. Now, to me pork is right-smart better than turkey. Turkey is dry meat anyway. I had missed the old gobblers, but I thought I would get me that whole hog, so I bought five shots. John Souders bought in, and John Conatzer, and my brothers George and Sam, and some of the other best shots, too.

That shore was a mean day. Them-there experts jes couldn't cut the centre out of their targets. They laid a whole mess of balls within an eighth of an inch of the centre, but that was not close enough to git the meat. I was still feeling bad about the turkeys and I wanted to git my whole five shots right through the centre; I had done it before and I figured I could do it agin. I figured on driving that hog home on the hoof. That was a trick of my father's. He would most often win all the prizes and drive the hog or beef home alive. But, like the others, I got all around the centre, but I couldn't cut it.

At last I put a ball inside of the other shots, it jes broke the centre, and then that-there young stripling of a Delk boy that had busted the turkey went and cut the centre right out of his target and got first prize He was the shootinest shooter of the whole bunch that day. I got second choice. They slaughtered and dressed the hog on the spot and I picked me a nice ham, which was not so bad after all.

John Conatzer didn't get none nohow, but he kinder consoled himself by saying that the pork would be sorter tough because it was killed in the soon of the moon—meaning, of course, when the moon was young. That's a mountain superstition.

Then we went back to finish off that last gobbler. He shore was the biggest one that ever come safely through Thanksgiving Day. John Souders remarked that he looked most as big as an ostrich. Jes as we were all gittin' ready to let fly at that last gobbler, a razorback sneaked in behind us and started in on George's dead turkey, which he had thronged down on the ground, and I am a-telling you, when George saw that hog calmly eating up his bird he let out a whoop like a red Indian. He started right after it, but the hog wasn't willing to let go. He picked up the turkey and lit out down the valley and over the hill and George kept a-going after him, and we all whooped and cheered, and finally George made a dive at the hog and the three of them went down in a heap, and there was feathers all over the place. But he got his turkey back, and when he returned he remarked that razorbacks never weren't good nohow.

Jes about this time Pastor Browne, who was holding a revival service in Jimtown, come out in the field. He is only a young man, but he looked jes like one of them thar old fire-eating pastors that used to preach fire and brimstone through these mountains in the old times. He was wearing a sort of square black hat and a sort of squared-off black suit, and he has a kind of square head and a square figure, and I guess he has a square mind; I mean he squares it with the Bible. He is a mighty powerful preacher and a right-smart pastor.

We invited him to bust the turkey's head. He hadn't handled a rifle for eight years, but he said he guessed he'd try. He wanted that turkey worser'n any of us, he guessed. Like a real preacher-man, he stood to one side and prayed to the Lord that if it was His will he would most awful like to have that turkey. He stepped right up to the mark, clapped the rifle to his shoulder, and prayed agin and then fired, and shore enough he busted the gobbler's head. It was the best turkey gobbler of the day, and his shooting was the straightest and the best, too. And when he got the turkey he told us that he didn't even see its head when he pointed the rifle. It was the prayer that done it. He was sure of that and we 'lowed maybe he was right.

Then he started for home in a hurry. The last we seed of him he was striding off across the hills, going back to Jimtown to hold his revival services that night. He looked about the happiest preacher man this side of Paradise. He was swinging the old turkey gobbler with one hand, and he was shouting praises to the Lord. Ho! ho!

CHAPTER 6

LARNIN' FROM NATURE

There are two kinds of larnin'-the larnin' you git out of books and the larnin' you pick up from living close to nature. If you could only git both you shore would be what they call educated. It's most hard, though. If you get one you seldom get the other. That's the way of things. Life's fair. There's a sort of balance in things. The people in the towns and cities get to larn from books and schools and people in this-here mountain country sorter got to larn from nature.

Larnin' to know trees and flowers and animals and sunsets is like readin' a big book. You have kinder got to go to school to understand that sort of readin'. I mean to a sort of outdoor school where you have got to tramp round, hunting and shooting, and stay out and use your eyes and your ears and your power of reasoning, too. What you pick up from these things sort of larns you a most awful lot about life. What you pick up from dogs and horses and foxes and squirrels and coons and bees and hornets, and the little critters in the earth, and most everything in the woods, helps you understand people, too.

I've got a lot of dogs around my farm. I know them and they know me. We kinder understand and love each other. A few months ago a boy up in Jimtown killed one of my dogs. I felt pretty bad about it. I jes kinder moped around and missed that dog for a considerable time. Oncet I had a coon dog that got into the most rip-roarin' fight with a big coon. He got scratched and beat up, but he stuck it out, and after he whipped the coon he came to me all full of hurt and wagged his tail and kinder twisted his bruised face into a sort of human smile, and then I kinder got down beside him and petted and hugged him. I jes couldn't help it.

And I have an English Walker. There is a dog for you. He is

pretty old now and getting grouchy but in his younger days I knowed him to trail a fox for forty hours without stopping. Then he'd come home, hungry and lame and worn out, and he would stand up and bark and whine and look at me with that knowing dog look in his eyes as though wondering if I was approving of what he'd done. I've got a couple of Red Bones, and when they git started after a fox they never stop. I'm a-telling you, you can larn a heap from dogs, and it makes you sort of more human to have them around.

Fox-hunting teaches you a lot. I ain't a-foolin' when I say that quite a heap of foxes have got a right-smart more sense than many human beings. The tricks they go in for to throw the hounds off the scent shore are astonishing. They circle and come back over their old trail. They go up creeks, jump from rock to rock, and walk along fences and rocks. They go in for all sorts of other contraptions; and they 'most always come home, too. They jes sorter circle away around for hours and sometimes for days, and then, sure enough, if they can throw off the hounds they come a-loping and a-sneaking back to their homes. Foxes think a heap more of their homes than a lot of humans do.

I kinder like laying out under the trees watching squirrels. They are the workinest animals. They are never still. They are always up and a-doing, picking nuts and whittling them to get the kernels out and storing them away against bad times; and feeding their young ones and teaching them to cling to trees and travel over the tops of the forests. They're kind of impudent, too, the way they chatter and scold. Squirrels sure have a heap of confidence in themselves and they're pretty tricky, too. They don't seem to mind you watching them, but they sure know when you've got a gun around.

But if you want to know what real courage and industry is, just tackle a hive of wild bees in a hollow tree on the mountainside. Ho! ho! They're right smart soldiers and they're the fightinest things. They're great believers in this-here "rights of self determination." When they come to swarming and buzzing around it ain't nobody's business to be too close. You may get the honey, but you're going to get a lot more, too, before the bees are finished with you. They're most awful intelligent too. If a mouse gets into their hive. Ho! Ho! They sting it to death and then seal hit off; that is, they seal it up in wax. They shore have a whole heap of sense. And talk about looking after their women folks! The way they fight and work for their queen is right smart. And when you try to rob their hives, the way they will all get around and try to hide her or get her away is a most astonishing thing. Bees are the hardest working, fiercest fighting, and most home-loving and sensible things in the forest.

There's a moth down here in the mountains that can even out-smart the bees. Hit goes into their hives and eats up the honey. That's looking for trouble, I'm a-telling you. But hit does it jes the same. Hit spins a sorter web around the entrance to the hive and gets in without the bees being able to get at it. Once inside it kinder webs itself off and eats up the honey; all of it in time. And the bees either starve to death or swarm somewhere else. That moth's what you might call a genius. Ho! ho!

Coons are brave and good fighters, but they ain't got so much sense. When the hounds git right after them instead of dodging and doubling on their trail and trying to hide away in the woods they climb plumb up the first tree; and then you have got them. When you cut the tree down, instead of trying to get away they cling to it until it crashes, and then they do the foolinest thing; they climb down the tree again to the butt before they jump to the ground. They sorter haven't realized that the tree is down, and that is jes plain ignorance. The hounds have got more sense. As soon as the tree falls they rush right to the butt; they jes know the coon is coming that way.

Hogs, too, ain't got over-much brains. They do the craziest things. They let the dogs most often run them into corners where they can scarcely turn around and can't get away nohow, and when the dog gets hold of them, they sorter stand there looking silly-like.

If you want to know what real happiness is jes wander out into the woods of a moonlight night and listen to the whipper-will singing. There is a bird for you, always good-natured, always happy, as if always glad for being borned. There is only one other bird that's like it. Hit's the mocking bird. There is a bird with a heap of sense and what you'd call imagination. Hits always kinder foolin' the other birds. There is folks here who say a mocking bird can make almost any sound and that some-times they can whistle almost like a man and that way fool a dog. I hain't never heard them do that myself, but I have heard them imitate other birds until you would think the forest was plumb full of almost every kind of bird. Hit is no ordinary bird that can do that. That's why I have always kind of thought a mocking bird the queen of all the birds in the forest.

You can larn a lot from birds and animals, but I kinder think you can larn most from the soil itself. I don't know much about philosophy. I am not certain that I know what it is. But I'm a-telling you that you do a heap of thinking about lots of things when you are following a plough and turning over great rows of all sorts of good soil. And somebody told me that Bobby Burns, the Scotch poet, used to make up a lot of his rhymes while ploughing and harrowing; so I went and read me that one about the mouse. That's poetry. Only a man who knows about the soil and the little critters in it could have written that. That's what I mean.

I kinder think that even if you can't write poems you can sorter think them; and when you're sitting on a harvester with the ripe, golden-headed wheat stalks waving at you and going down as you go along, your mind sorter fills up and brims over, and all sorts of beautiful thoughts kinder sing in your soul.

I guess we have all got a little of this-here poetry in us and it takes old Mother Nature to bring it out. That's the way with me anyhow.

I am most awful fond of the woods after it's been raining. I like to stand in them and swing my arms and take deep breaths. There's scents there that jes make your soul bob with joy. And as for pictures, I ain't never seen none that could come up to a sunset in our valley, when the sky out there in the west is that full of colours that you sorter get drunk on them. And if you have never seen the woods when they are full of moonlight, all sorter soft and milky, you ain't never seen nothing nohow.

I am a-telling you you can larn a lot from nature. I ain't an artist nor a poet nohow. I don't know much about pictures and poems. I often don't understand them when I read or see them. But I kinder got a hankering after these-here natcheral things. I may be all wrong, but somehow, way inside of me, I kinder feel the best poems have never been written and never will be, and I jes know the best pictures in the world can never be made with paints and brushes.

I have been a heap criticized for what I done when I come back from the war; for turning down all themthere offers to go on the stage and into the movies and in business. I knowed I was turning down fortunes, I knowed I could never hope nohow to make a lot of money like that agin. But I couldn't help it.

Even at that-there big banquet in New York City I jes couldn't help thinking about them-there hound dogs of mine. I kinder heard them baying and calling and I couldn't get back to them quick enough. I seed the lights of Broadway. I liked them. But I jes knowe'd they didn't mean as much to me as the stars and the moonlight and that-there little valley and the growin' crops and woods and flowers at home. So I jes natcherly lit out on the first train.

I love being out-of-doors. I jes love it. I am used to it, and all my people, way back to old Coonrod Pile, and I am a-thinking away back beyond him too, loved being out and foolin' around where there was plenty of room to move in. I suppose everybody jes has different fancies. I ain't even questioning that. I ain't even a-saying people are wrong for liking the cities and the bright lights and the noises-if they get the most enjoyment out of them, it's all right with me. But I don't. And so I turned my back on them; and I am back here on the farm with my own people, in the mountains I love. I jes couldn't hope to be happy if I couldn't hunt and shoot and tramp around these-here hills with them-there hound dogs of mine.

I have got five of them, three English hounds and two Red Bones. The English hounds are good for most anything you want them for. They're the most usable dogs. They're good for squirrels, coons, foxes, razorbacks and even rabbits. The ' Red Bones are no good for nothing except foxes. They won't yelp after nothing but foxes, but once they pick up the scent they sure will follow until they catch the animals, or get them back into their den.

The best coon dogs, though, has got to be trained for the job. They have got to be taught that they must follow a scent without yelping, because if they make a heap of noise the coon will hear them and keep a-going and never come near enough to be treed. You have got to understand dogs before you can get much hunting out of them. You have got to understand their ways and what they're good for, and you have got to understand the habits of the things they're hunting, too.

CHAPTER 7

RIGHT-SMART HUNTER

To be a right-smart hunter you have got to know not only about guns and hounds and woods and animals, but the right kind of clothes to wear. You have got to be comfortable when you are in the woods or tramping over the hills. You can't enjoy a hunt and you can't shoot straight or keep up with the hounds unless you are feeling all right. I have missed easy shots from being wet through and cold when I should not have been. And the wrong kind of socks or boots have made me miss more'n one fox or coon. I 'most always wear overalls and a hunting coat made of waterproof ducking. I wear light leggings and light hobnail boots and a good shady hat.

My favourite hunting is after fox. I don't mean riding the hounds. I mean following the hounds on foot, or sort of going acrost the circle to where you know they're most likely to be and getting them as they go by. You have shore got to know the habits of foxes and you have got to have good hounds and be a fair-to-middling shot if you hope to have any sort of success at this sort of sport.

We have two kinds of foxes here, the red and the gray. The red will run for two or three days before it circles back to its den, but the gray ones only take a few hours. When we go out after foxes we sorter hike along until the dogs hit the trail. Then they begin to bay. That's music, I'm a-telling you. We then get on top of a ridge where we can sort of locate things. We can most always tell whether it's a red or a gray fox by the size of the circle they're running. The gray keeps in kinder close, but the red goes from mountain to mountain and on through the gaps mile after mile. It shore takes a lot to tire them.

If we know it is a gray fox we go over on the edge of the plantation or on a bluff. It has a habit of making for those sort of places. If it is a red one we hide in the gaps in the mountains where we know it is most sure to go. Them-there red foxes is runners. They sure know how to wear the padding off'n a hound's feet and then lead him home all tired out. They sure enough are "dog tired" when they run a red fox. Foxes are very sly. They can see and smell a long way, and if the hounds catch up with them they will fight too.

Coon-hunting is 'most always at night. A dark night, or when there is about a quarter moon, is the best. It is good sport, if you have the right kind of dog. A coon lives in the woods, generally around the heads of the hollows. He feeds on corn, acorns, and chestnuts and the like. You take your coon dog out in the hills and turn him loose and you seldom hear of him again until he begins to bay. Then you know he's treed a coon. If it is in small timber sometimes you can shake the coon out and let him fight it out with the dogs. A coon's a good, hard fighter, much better'n a cat. It takes a right-smart dog to whip a coon. If you can't shake him out you have got to get busy with axe and saws and cut down the tree. That is, of course, if you want the sport; but if you don't care for the sport and only want the coon, you can shoot him out; that is, if it is not too dark and you can see him; and if it is dark, you can get out your electric pocket torch and shine the light around the tree until it reflects in the coon's eyes. He 'most always is looking down at you or the dogs. Then you can shoot with a fair chance of getting him. I have often stayed out all night and slept under the tree. It was too dark to see him and I didn't have a pocket torch or an axe along with me, so I jes had to stay with them dogs until the morning when it was light again and I could get me the coon.

Mountain cats are right-smart fighters, too, but the dogs don't seem to care. They rush in and soon kill them. I have knowed some cats that weighed forty or fifty pounds. I don't like cats. They ain't no sports nohow and when they get after lambs and pigs they shore cost a heap of money.

Hog-hunting is a favourite sport in the mountains. I have

been in a heap of wild-hog hunts. The wild hogs around here are mostly domestic hogs that have been turned out and have sorter gone back on their kind. We keep hogs in the woods all the time. They get fat on the acorns, beechnuts, hickory nuts, and chestnuts. They jes grub around and find them or dig them up and have a right-smart time. Sometimes as many as fifty different farmers have their hogs running in the same woods. We all mark them with our own particular mark and fasten bells on straps around the necks of the leaders.

When a hog goes wild his whole nature seems to change. He lies up in the daytime and runs wild during the night, which is jes the opposite to the tame hogs. When we go hunting for them we trail them with our dogs, and then when the dogs bay them we go up and let loose a specially trained hound, which gets them by the leg and holds them or even throws them. I once knowed a dog, a sort of half bulldog he was. He used to grip the hog by the nose and then jes lie down. That shore was a sight and he wouldn't let loose nohow. The fool old hog would jes stand there and shake his head, and not know what to do. Hogs shore ain't got much sense. We generally shoot the wild hogs with our old muzzle-loaders. That's why we call them hog rifles.

Squirrel-hunting is pretty good. It's best in the fall when the woods is full of hickory nuts. The best way to get them is to locate your hickory trees, and then go in among them early in the morning. You have got to know how to slip in quietly and not disturb a leaf or twig. You have got to understand, to know the feel and sort of sense what I call the sounds of the forest. And in the forest every sound, every flutter of a leaf, every falling of a nut, every strip of bark fluttering down, everything means something.

The forest has its own way of talking. It has a language of its own, and the hunter jes has got to understand and learn that-there language, and he has got to keep his eyes and ears open all the time, especially if he is out after squirrels. If you know these things and act natcheral you can go right in among the squirrels. I have seen as many as twenty in one tree. They set up there on the branches, whittling the nuts. They whittle off a hole and then they get the kernel out. They eat mulberries, acorns, chestnuts, and beech and hickory nuts. They eat the buckeye too. Part of that is very poisonous, but I am a-telling you the squirrel knows that. He knows which part to eat and which part to leave. Some animals shore have a lot of sense.

This country shore used to be full of deer, but they have been 'most shot out and there are only a few left. I have only shot a few deer, and I don't know much about it.

I don't know much about baar-hunting either. There's a few baars left, but they are back in the mountains and it's hard to get at them. It's more luck than skill, getting a baar in these mountains these days. A few weeks ago one of our mountain boys was driving a truck acrost a trestle bridge when he almost run p'int-blank into a baar which was going acrost the bridge from the other direction. That-there old baar jes kept a-going on. Hit warn't scared of that-there old motor truck nohow. So the boy went into reverse and backed up and give that old baar the right-of-way. That's sportsmanship for you. He jes warn't going to run plumb into that old baar and probably go over into the creek below. As he himself has said, baars are scarce enough, but if you have got the time and patience you can go into the mountains and get one, but you can't get another truck that way nohow.

The most exciting sport of all is cutting down a bee tree. I am a-telling you that's looking for punishment. Some men can get along with bees. I can't nohow. My brother Henry can handle them with his bare hands and do 'most anything with them; and they very rarely sting him, and when they do, it don't seem to bother him much. But they sort of have a natcheral dislike for me. They come at me right smart, and they shore make me do all these-here funny dances all over the mountain. Wild hogs are mean fighters and they often kill our dogs. Baars have got a bad way with them and coons and mountain cats ain't at all sociable, but the worst of them all are them-there wild bees. It kinder beats me how such a little critter can do so much damage when he sorter backs up against you and pushes.

But we mountain people are most fond of the honey and we will go to any length to get it. We hunt the wild bees jes like, we hunt 'most any other animal, except, of course, we don't use dogs. A dog has got even less business than a human around a wild beehive. We put out bee bait on the trees. We generally use burnt sugar, or honey, or something else that's sweet. The bees come along and get at it and then we try and follow them up to their bee tree. They generally hive in a big hollow tree on the high ground on top of a mountain.

Once we have the tree located we begin making preparations. We sometimes get all dressed up. We wear bee bonnets, which are made out of something like mosquito netting, draped down over our hats and tucked into the collars of our coats. We wear gloves and thick woollen socks, or leggings. But, somehow or other, wild bees when you rob their hives know how to penetrate most any clothing. They sure find the open places, and then—ho! ho! But 'most all of the mountain boys, though they don't like bee stings nohow, generally go out without dressing in them-there special clothes. But they sure take a lot of punishment. My brother Sam tackled a hive oncet, and by the time he had felled the tree he was so wet with sweat that his clothes were jes clinging to him and the bees most nigh drove him off before he could even get near the honey.

The other night we cut down a bee tree and got one of the biggest hauls of honey we have ever known. We got out over two big bucketfuls, and there was even more'n that spilt or mussed up. It was a great big half-hollow oak tree on one of the mountains about three miles through the woods. We had a most awful time getting in over the rough places, sliding down mountains and climbing up others, and getting all tangled up in vines and thorny brushes. It was a very tall tree. We sawed it down. We tried to fall it on a small cedar so as not to smash up the trunk and spill the honey, but the cedar gave way, and that old tree cracked up and there was honey and bees all over the place.

I kept well back and held the dog. I don't like bee stings nohow. Besides, that-there dog thought it was a coon tree and was rarin' to go. He would have rushed in there and stuck his nose into the honey and the bees would have stung every square inch of him. It's right-smart funny, I am a-telling you, to see a hound howling and prancing around, rubbing his nose with his paws, but it's cruel jes the same, and it don't do the hound no good nohow. So I clung to mine, and later on I tied him to a sapling.

When the tree crashed the boys run along beside the trunk until they located the hive. You couldn't miss it nohow. It was jes a wild, mad swarm of mad bees, and the sweetest, most golden honey you ever tasted. My brother Henry turned in with his bare hands and didn't seem to mind the bees nohow. My other brothers, Jim and Sam, went in with him, but in a few minutes they come out again, and they agreed that bees never was no good nohow. Jim was so badly stung around the ankles that he couldn't get his shoes on next day. Worse than that, he was biting into a piece of honeycomb and there was a bee in it and it bit him on the end of the tongue and he hollered worse'n a baar. Sam jes kinder sneaked out and got well out of the firing line. He didn't want to admit that the bees had whipped him, but they had jes the same.

But that-there Henry stayed with them. You could hardly see him for the bees and honey. He filled himself full and said it was the best he had ever tasted. Then he filled the buckets and the cans and a cardboard box, and there was a lot more running out and jes as much was lost as was ketched. Henry always kinder believed that when you are robbing a hive you are safer in the swarm than on the outside. He says the fighters always skirmish on the outside and go right after anybody who's straggling around, but if you are in among them, and especially if you have honey on you, they won't touch you unless you happen to squeeze or pinch them, and then they let fly with them-there torpedoes. They crawled all over Henry and he jes lightly brushed or pulled them off and kept right on after the honey. And then he poked about among the bees looking for the queen. That stirred them up, but he didn't seem to mind. That-there Henry is the foolishest man that ever took honey out of a hive. He don't seem to mind bees at all, and their stings don't seem to bother him nohow.

After they had kinder recovered from the effects of the first attack, Jim and Sam sorter slunk back in among them, but their confidence was sorter ruined. It don't take many bee stings to do that. But no stings no honey, and they wanted more honey, and they got it, and everything else that went with it. In the evening we carried those old buckets and cans full of honey back home. The next day we went out and rounded up the bees. We wanted to take them home, too. We took a gum along with us. That is a sort of box-shaped beehive. We looked around for the queen, to put her in the gum, but them-there bees sure were on the warpath and we couldn't find her nohow. We put some of the comb we had left in the box and let it stand there and went away and when we come back again they was swarming in the box and we was able to take them home and they're on the farm now. Bees sure have a lot of sense.

So I have growed up hunting and shooting and larning a few of the secrets of nature in these forests and mountains. And I'm a-telling you, you can larn a lot that way.

CHAPTER 8

Saddlebag Preachers

The old-timers in these-here mountains sure must have believed that "man cannot live by bread alone." I mean whiskey alone, ho! ho! They had to have religion and they done had it. But jes as they couldn't git in over the bad roads and across the creeks to school, they often couldn't git in to church. So the church had to go to them. And it done went, at least the saddle baggers went.

I'm a-tellin' you that them-there old Presbyterian and Methodist and Baptist preacher-men played a right-smart part in civilizing the people of the mountains. They were called saddlebaggers because of the big saddlebags they carried on their horses. They stuffed these bags with Bibles, song books, and religious magazines, which they sold or give out wherever they done went. The people in the mountains thought jes as much of their religion, and a little more, too, than they thought of their fighting and hunting, and they was most awful fond of them saddlebaggers. The Scotch-Irish, Scotch Cavaliers, Lutherans, and Huguenots who pioneered this country were most awful religious people. But they believed in their own and not in other people's gods. That's why they lit out from the other side and come over here and takened on to the wilderness rusher than to live in comfort in their own homes. They knowed that over here they could find that political and religious liberty they were looking for. Even to this day you won't find many rosaries or Episcopalian prayer books in these-here mountains, and you won't find many rituals or liturgies either. The mountain people don't like them nohow. They don't permit anything except the Bible to stand between them and their God. They sorter like their religion plain, like their ancestors did and like the old Prophets did.

But they were so busy fighting and making their homes that they had no time nohow to do much preaching themselves. Then the saddlebaggers come. They was pioneers themselves, farmers, blacksmiths, gunsmiths, and hunters. They was jes plain people, earning their living by the sweat of their brow. But they felt the spirit of God telling them to go out among their fellowmen and preach His word. So of a Saturday and Sunday, and sometimes for weeks, they would git in the saddle and stuff their old saddlebags full of Bibles and hymn books and go a-ridin' through the mountains. If there was mountain churches they would hold their services there. If there was no churches they would hold them in the schoolhouse; and if there was no schoolhouse they would hold them in the cabins on the mountainside. Wherever they could get a few people together they would have a preaching. There was never a mountain cabin too far back for them to call at. There was never a family too poor for them to visit. They regarded all people alike as the children of God and themselves as His blessed messengers.

They not only held meetings everywhere they went, but they baptized and held marriage services and comforted the sick and buried the dead. They received very little salary or none at all. Preaching was not a profession or a business with them like it so often is now. It was the work of God. They looked forward to their reward in the next world. They was good men, sincere preachers. They worked most hard. They traveled through all sorts of weather, winter and summer. They rode over the worstest roads, up creek beds, over the mountains. They were greatly loved and respected by all the people, and though they never carried arms they were never touched. They used to stay at whatever mountain cabin they arrived at nightfall, and they was always welcome, too. They were close preachers; that is, they clung closer to the word of God as it is written in the Bible than a coon to a tree when a hound-dog has chased him up there. They were what we would call fire-and-brimstone preachers.They believed in the reward of heaven for the good and the punishment of hell for the wicked. And I'm a-tellin' you theirs was the finest heaven there ever was and theirs was the worstest hell. They shore knowed all about the pearly gates and the everlasting flames.

There was many famous saddlebaggers riding circuits in these-here mountains. Jackie Brown was one of them. He come from somewhere over in North Carolina and sorter made his headquarters in our valley, and from here he would ride out through the mountains preaching and taking the word of God to the furtherest corners. Often he was the first preacher that the settlers away back in the mountains had ever seen. Sometimes he got so far back in that he found people that had never even seed a Bible before. Oncet at a famous meeting near Wolf River, in the valley, he said he would be happy to die at any time if he thought that by so doing he could save jes one lost soul. He meaned it, too, and the people listening knowed he meaned it.

About seventeen years later another preacher man named Bobby Burke come along with a new religion of the Gospel of Sanctification. He converted Jackie Brown to his new religion, and when Jackie was saved, as he called it, he told the congregation that he was awful glad that he hadn't died before, because if he had done so he shore would hare gone straight to hell.

Jackie was saved between the saddle and the ground, so he used to say. It come to him sudden. He had been to a meeting and heard Bobby Burke preach and he was riding over to Jasper Pile's to get his dinner when he felt the power moving him and he knowed he was sanctified. He got off of his horse and laid on the flat of his back on the dusty road and slapped his hands and begun to holler. A man by the name of Jack Frogge was going down the road at the time, and when he saw Jackie Brown he thought it was some man drunk or crazy, and so he takened out around the other side and lit out for home and never stopped until he got there.

When Jackie Brown got up he run his hands into his pockets and pulled out his plug of tobacco and thronged it into the woods, and then he done went home to his farm, where he had half an acre of tobacco growing, and he takened a hoe and hacked it down and threw it over the fence. He said if it was not right for him to use tobacco it was not right for him to grow it and sell it to other people. His neighbours got after him and said that as he was poor he should have kept the tobacco and marketed it. But he said the Lord would not let him starve. They say he become a most powerful fine preacher after he was sanctified.

Another well-known saddlebagger was a man named Adams. He was blind. He couldn't look out into the world, but he declared he could look into people's souls. He was much loved and respected, as he should have been. They say that he was a Southerner and a very wonderful fellow. At about the same time that he was preachin' another saddlebagger by the name of Sam Greer come into the valley. He was a Northerner and a fire-eater. Long after the Civil War this Ahere Greer and Adams come together at a revival meeting on Wolf River. Sam Greer plumb forgot that he was a preacher man and he lit into Adams most awful for being a Rebel and a Southerner. So you see that often these saddlebaggers were human like most other people. They had their likes and dislikes. I'm a-thinking that is why they was so well received and loved wherever they went.

The most famous of the saddlebaggers was Ab Wright. There was a man for you! He "rowed up in our valley and rode through these-here mountains for nigh onto fifty years. He is a-resting in his grave now, but I'm a-telling you his memory still lives in the hearts of the old-timers around here. They never tire of talking about him and his wonderful sermons and long rides and the great good he done. Tennessee was a pretty tough place around seventy five year ago when he begun carrying the word of God around. The roads were jes mountain trails. There were few bridges. Towns and even mountain cabins were a right-smart piece apart; and often Ab Wright was out all night in the cold and the rain on the mountainside. Agin and agin he was near drowned or bewatered by some sudden rising of creek or river.

Oncet he was lost in the wilderness. He was not like old Daniel Boone, who said he was never lost in the forest but he was once bewildered for a few days. He really was lost and he didn't know where he was nohow, and he had to do a most awful lot of praying before he found the road. Another time he was feeding a large herd of cattle when he was gored by a mad bull. It tossed him several times and he come near to losing his life. And worst of all, he was bit by a copperhead. He put his hand down in a sheaf of oats and the serpent got him on the wrist. It made him most awful sick, but he didn't lose his head. He bound his wrist above the wound to keep the poison from spreading, and then kept sucking the bite and spitting out the poison until he was a heap better; but jes the same he was not getting well nohow.

In them days they didn't know much about snake medicine, so they jes put another bandage on his arm, tighter than the first, to make shore the poison wouldn't spread. This bandage was so tight that it kinder cut off circulation and his shoulder and neck become so swollen that he couldn't hardly breathe; and then they begun to give him whiskey. That was about the only remedy that the mountaineers knowed for snake bite, and I guess hit was a pretty doubtful cure at that. He drunk three pints of raw whiskey in a few minutes, and then, so he said afterwards, he felt pretty drowsy and went to sleep—and while he was sleeping the whiskey and the poison fought it out inside of him and the whiskey won.

Next morning when he come to he was out of danger, but he shore was most awful sick—from the snake bite—ho! ho! For three seasons after that in the springtime, so he said, the bitten arm changed to the color of a serpent and shed off the outside skin. But he come round all right and was able to continue his preaching to the end of his life.

Ab Wright was a most awful good man. He had good word to say for everybody, even for the criminals. Oncet he was praying with a condemned man the whole of his last night on this earth. It was in Jimtown. The man was James Calvin Logstone. He was sentenced to hang for killing two women and a child with an axe. Ab Wright was with him most all of the last twenty-four hours. He done went and prayed with him in the cell and comforted him all he could. Well, when they were ready to hang him they put him in a shroud and placed him on a wagon with his coffin. Ab Wright and the doctor set beside him, and a heavy guard surrounded them all. They rode to the gallows, singing hymns as they went. The death warrant was read and Ab Wright preached the funeral service. He must have converted the condemned man, too, because after he done shaken hands with the people he told them he done come to his end through keeping bad company and warned them to keep away from the like. Then they stringed him up, but the rope broke and he fell to the ground. They got another rope and placed it around his neck and he was drawn up agin, but after a few moments the rope broke agin and he fell to the ground for the second time. Maybe they ought to have let him go then, but they didn't. They jes lifted him up agin, and as they done so he said a few words, but nobody knowed what they was. This time the rope didn't break and he hung twenty-five minutes and was pronounced dead. All through this terrible time Ab Wright and some other preacher men were there, singing hymns and praying to the Lord.

In one year this most wonderful old saddlebagger preached one hundred and eighty-one times, received one hundred and five persons into the Church, prayed with five hundred families, baptized fifty-four people and traveled over two thousand miles on horseback over the mountain country. He received no salary for this and only took up a few bits of collections. And during this year he had to look after his farm. That's a preacher man for you. In his whole life he baptized one thousand three hundred and twenty-three people, married eighty-seven couples, and held six hundred and eleven burial services. I know that our preacher men today do a lot of work, and most of them are sincere and godly men, but when I think of Ab Wright doing all of this in the mountains years ago when traveling was much harder and living was much worse than it is today, and never caring nohow whether he got paid or not, I kinder feel that him and the preacher men like him was among the anointed of the Lord.

Pastor Pile—Rosier Pile, we call him—who keeps a store to this day at Pall Mall and has a Sunday-school class too, used to be a saddlebagger. He used to ride through the mountains a-prayin' and holdin' meetings and a-visitin'. And he never received no salary neither and he didn't want none.

But jes like the feuds and the bushwhackers, these here grand old saddlebaggers of the past are disappearing. Roads are coming into the mountains and people can get into church, and even if they can't go in they can build small churches a heap easier than before. So the preacher man on horseback with his saddlebags full of Bibles and religious books is passing out. There are a few of them left. These here modern times that are with us are sorter silencing "the voice crying in the wilderness."

CHAPTER 9

Mother

Like most all boys, I think my mother was the best mother in all the world. I jes think so much of her that I don't know how to say what I want to say. I guess sometimes you can feel things so deep you are sorter lost for words to express them.

We mountain people are pretty clannish; that's the Scotch-Irish blood in us. We sorter hang together, 'most like bees when they are swarming. I sometimes think that our feelings are nearer the surface than they are in 'most all city people. We don't try to keep them down. We let them go. When we love we love right out, and we ain't ashamed of it, and when we hate it takes a lot to make us forgive and forget.

Both my father and mother were honest, God-fearing people, and they did their best to bring us up that way. They didn't drink, or swear, or smoke themselves, and they didn't believe in us doing those things. They didn't have no use nohow for people who told lies or broke promises. They believed in being straight out and aboveboard. I'm a-telling you they honoured the truth so much that they wouldn't hide it nohow for nobody even if they was to suffer an awful lot. I have told about my father. It was sorter easy for me to talk about guns and hounds and horses and all those things he loved and taught me to love. Hit's different talking about Mother, but I jes got to. Her story is jes sorter mixed up with mine and mine with hers, and I can't jes tell where one ends and the other begins, and I can't look into my own life nohow without finding her always mixed up with my affairs. And always for the better. I have generally taken her advice as being most helpful. When I have failed to do it, I have 'most always got into a heap of trouble. I can't remember us ever having a short word.

She has sort of been through everything. She has had ‘most all the trials and tribulations they write about in the Scriptures. She has always had to work hard, and she says that is why she has always been happy. I guess she has never really had time to be unhappy. I am a-thinking that she sorter knows what life’s all about. Long ago she had come through most all of the fool notions, and she sorter understands now.

When her father, William Brooks, was killed by the bushwhackers in Jamestown, she was jes a little baby in her mother’s arms. Her brother was not borned then. He come into the world a few months afterwards. The three of them went on through life clinging to each other jes like a three-leaf clover. My grandmother never married again. She jes went back to her people in the valley and give her whole life to bringing up her babies. She had to be both mother and father to them. Maybe it’s because my mother never had a father she growed up so independent and strong-willed and knowing. She had to larn to look after herself without a father and to find out heaps of things alone.

There was no man-person at the house and they all had to work, and her little brother was sickly at first. She went to school and larned how to read and write and that was about all. She never read no other books but the Bible. She larned to card and spin and weave and knit and to make clothes. She milked the cows and even larned how to plough. She used to hitch up the horses and go out into the field and do a good day’s work. She had some cattle of her mother’s, and she often used to go out in the fields and hitch them to logs and do her share of hauling. She worked right smart from her girlhood up.

She must have been full of life, too. I’m a-telling you she still is. She used to go in for all the goings-on in the valley. In those old days there was a lot of this what you would call community spirit. If a couple would marry and wanted to set up for themselves, or if some strangers come in and takened up some land, most all of the mountain people around would turn out and give them a good start. There would be log-rollings and house-raisings. The men would do that. They would come from all around and cut the timber and roll in the logs and clear up the brush and burn it off, so that the new settlers would have some good crop land. Then they would build them a home, a regular log cabin; and while they was doing this, the women folk would get together and do, a right-smart piece of quilting. That is, they would cut and sew and make quilts and other things for the new couple to help begin a home.

And after the day's work was, done they would all get together and dance on the new puncheon floor. They would often dance all night, them square dances with banjo music and fiddles. They jes paired up and hit the floor, the young and old, married and single, and all. The men sometimes would drink a little hard cider and liquor but they seldom got drunk.

Then there were corn-shuckings too. Somebody would put up a crib of corn and maybe put a bottle of liquor in the centre. The men folks would come in from all around and shuck until they got right in the centre where the liquor was. Then there would be some drinking, and after that there would be some dancing. In them days they all worked hard from sunup to sundown; and they knowed how to play, too. Their enjoyments might be different from ours, but they was kinder wholesome and sorter fitted in with this-here mountain life.

Roads were bad in them times and travelling was hard. Anyone who went into Jimtown more'n once a month was considered to be a regular gad-about. The first time my mother ever went into Jimtown she drove a yoke of cattle with a load of fodder. It was a little place then, but it was a new world for her, for she had been used only to the little mountain place. They used to raise sorghum cane in them days and grind the stalks into molasses and cut the heads off, and then they would take them heads that was left and fill up the, bottom of the cart and then pile up bundles of fodder on top until the cart was full. It was a load like this that she took into Jimtown.

Mother and Father most growed up together. They both lived in this-here valley. They first got to going together when my father decided to move house and Mother did the moving for him. This was long before they were married. They was both most young then. She took her cattle and wagon and went and moved him from off the mountain where he was living to his new place, which was within shouting distance of her own home. She drove the oxen and he walked along the road, toting a rifle, with a dog following him. That was the beginning of it.

They had to run off to be married. You see her people were opposed to him. They jes couldn't see him nohow, so they went and eloped. They ran across the mountains to her uncle's. He was a squire and in them days the squire could issue a licence and marry people himself. He married them. Mother's wedding dress was made of mixed linsey. She spun the wool, wove the cloth, and made the dress herself. They stayed over at her uncle's for a week. They spent their honeymoon helping the old people. Then when they kinder figured that Grandmother had got over her fractiousness, they returned.

About a year later Father built the log house at the spring, and that's where most all of us were horned and growed up. The children kept coming right smart until there were eleven of us. Mother had to work hard from sunup often until ten o'clock at night to keep us clothed and fed. Of course, Father had his black smithing and was the head of the house, but thirteen's a big family, and there just couldn't be no idle hands nohow. Until we was old enough to help, Mother had to do 'most everything around the house. She milked the cows, made the butter; she looked after the hogs and chickens. She made the soap and the tallow candles and fixed the grease for the lamps. She carded the wool and spun and wove the cloth and made all of our clothes. She was a good mother to us, and with Father she brought us all up, and we are living to-day. We're all strong and healthy and well and she enjoyed every moment of it. She enjoyed life much more in those days, so she says, slaving and working for us, than she does to-day, Jes quietly living with us with not much to do or to bother about.

She jes didn't have time to worry or be unhappy. Life tried to crowd in on her and bust her up right smart and she jes wouldn't let it nohow. She knowed what she wanted-she wanted her home, her husband, and her own children, and she knowed she would have to pay for these things with work and sacrifice, so she was willing. That's a mother for you! And that's what she's done done for me.

And here I was running hog-wild around the country, keeping her up late nights and worrying the heart out of her. No matter how long I stayed away and how late I come home, no matter how drunk I wag, no matter how much I had gambled away my money, no matter how much I come home shouting and whooping it up, she never had a short word for me, never. She would shake her head and look at me, with a hurt look in her eyes, and sometimes she would cry and always she would beg me to give it up and lead a better life. Sometimes I would come home from a big drunk or from a wild party, and I would find her sitting up in the lamp light waiting for me. And when I would ask her why she hadn't laid down or gone to bed, she would kinder look at me and say she couldn't sleep, because she was afraid I would get killed or something would happen to me.

Often she would remind me of my father, of how he never drunk, or gambled, or played around with bad company, and of how he would not like it nohow if he knowed what I was doing; and she used to meet me at the door and put her arms around me and tell me that I was not only wasting this life, but I was spoiling all my chances for the next. She used to say that she jes couldn't bear to think of where I would go if I died or was killed while I was leading this wild life.

All of this was making me feel kinder bad. I jes knowed I was wrong. I jes knowed there was no excuse for me, and I was beginning to make up my mind to cut it out, when she begun her praying for me. She told me of the Good Shepherd in the Bible who left the whole flock of sheep to go and look after and bring in the one that had strayed. She prayed and prayed. So I made up my mind to finish it. It was hard though. When you get used to a thing, no matter how bad it is for you, it is most awful hard to give it, up.

It was a most awful struggle to me. I did a lot of walking through the mountains and thinking. I was fighting the thing inside of me and it was the worstest fight I ever had. I thought of my father and what a good man he was and how he expected me to grow up like him, and I sorter turned over in my mind all the sacrifices Mother had made for me. I ricollected that I had never asked her to do anything which she refused if it was right. I knowed that she had given up 'most all of her life for her children. I knowed she would have given her whole life for me. I knowed how she loved me. And now she was asking me to give up all of this wild life and bad companions and be a good boy again.

So I thought and struggled and prayed more and more. And then, jes as I was making up my mind and getting control of myself, a preacher-man come into the valley. He was the Rev. H. H. Russell from Indiana. He preached very close. I mean very close to the word of God as it is revealed in the Bible. He fought everything that any preacher could have fought. He fought everything that was not right. His meetings were at the Wolf River Church. The people come in from all around. They come from the river flats and from the back creeks and from the mountains. They come most in farm wagons and on horseback, and some of them walked. It was a wonderful crowd. The church could scarcely hold them all. There were great meetings every night, and that preacher man had more conversions, in the time, than any other man that had ever been through the valley.

Sometimes I used to walk out on the mountainside and do a heap of thinking and praying before the meetings. Then I would go and listen and pray and ask God to forgive me for my sins and help me to see the light. And He did. In that-there little church, out in the hills and at home with Mother, I begun to see how wrong I was and how terrible it was for a man to be wasting his life like I was. I begun to see that I was missing the finer things. I knowed in my heart that when you miss the finer things of life you might jes as well be a razorback out in the mountains for all the good you are to yourself and anybody else.

So I decided to change and go in for the finer things. And I have done it. I give up smoking, drinking, gambling, cussing, and brawling. I give them up completely and forever. I give them up the first of January, 1, 1915. I have never backslided. I have never done any of those things since. I have no desire any more. I am a great deal like Paul, the things I once loved I now hate. I went through the World War without drinking, smoking, or cussing.

After I changed my life everybody around me was happy. My mother was most happy of all. I found out the truth of what the Bible. says: "There is more rejoicing over one sinner that repenteth than over ninety-nine just persons that need no repentance." But I was not yet saved. I knew there was something else. I continued to pray and go to church, and then it come to me that not only must a man not do bad, but he must also do good to be truly saved. I joined the church. It was called the Church of Christ in Christian Union. It hasn't any rituals or anything like that. Its only creed is the Bible. It accepts the Bible as it is written. I gave most of my spare time to it, and with Pastor Pile I helped teach a children's class at Sunday school. I also led the singing. I have a natural tenor voice. I went to Byrdstown and takened lessons. I became known as the Singing Elder.

So I was saved!

And that is the greatest victory I ever won. It's much harder to whip yourself than to whip the other fellow, I'm a-telling you, and I ought to know because I done, both. It was much harder for me to win the great victory over myself than to win it over those German machine guns in the Argonne Forest. And I was able to do it because my mother's love led me to God, and He showed me the light, and I done followed it.

CHAPTER 10

War is A-Brewin'

Life tol'ably queer. You think you've got a grip on it, then you open your hands and you find there's nothing in them. It doesn't go in straight lines like bees to their hives or quail from the covey. It sorter circles like foxes and goes back again to where it begun. After I had given up liquoring and gambling and fighting and the wild life, I kinder thought I could settle down in peace and make amends for my sins by working hard and doing all the good I could. I got me a job farming with Rosier Pile. I worked from sunup to sundown. I kept up my singing lessons, and I spent any spare time I had reading the Bible and doing church work.

Of course, often the old longing to go out and bedevil around would come over me, but I jes prayed and resisted the temptation. Sometimes Everett or Marion or some of the other boys would drop around and tell me they were putting on another gay party and invite me to join them. Then it was that I was most sorely tempted. I prayed most awful hard and got a good hold on myself and didn't go. Each time I refused, it was so much easier next time; and everyday it became easier. In a few months I got them there bad things out of my mind. I was thinking of better things, more worthwhile things. I was beginning to find peace in my soul.

So I was happy, living and working and learning to love my fellowmen and trying most awful hard to help anybody that wanted help. My mother was nigh to the happiest woman in the valley. She was always smiling and putting her hands on my shoulder sorter loving-like whenever I was around. That made me feel good. Most all of my friends were glad too. That encouraged me. I worked harder than ever. I read the Bible. I led the singing in the church, and I helped in the Sunday school.

I jes knowed I was saved.

I truly felt as though I had been borned again. I felt that great power which the Bible talks about and which all sinners feel when they have found salvation. I felt in my soul like the stormy waters must have felt when the Master said, "Peace, be still." I used to walk out in the night under the stars and kinder linger on the hillside, and I sorter wanted to put my arms around them-there hills. They were at peace and so was the world and so was I.

And, of course, there was a girl; a little slip of a girl. I knowed her since she was a baby. We sorter growed up together. She was younger than me, and it may have been on account of that or because I was careless and didn't notice things, when I was drinking and sinning around-anyway, I hadn't noticed how she had growed up from girlhood to womanhood. But when I was saved and working hard and going in for the decent things again, I begun to watch her comings and goings pretty close. I didn't see much of her at first. I guess she had heard of my wild life and sorter wasn't interested and kept out of my way, but when I got religion the church work brought us together. We did not speak to each other much at first. She was kinder shy; she hain't never been out of the mountains and hain't been used to strangers. But she had a nice way about her, always kind to folks and always doin' things for the church. There hain't been nothing flighty about her nohow. And I'm a-tellin' you she was pretty, always as fresh as a flower in the mornin' with the dew on. I kinder noticed her hair. You jes couldn't help noticing it. I jes couldn't nohow. It was sort of soft and silky and there was so much of it, and she done it up nice in two big braids wound up in the back with a blue ribbon woven in. And I seed her eyes was blue and big and kinder shined with goodness, and though I never thought of it before, I jes knowed blue was my favourite colour. I am a-tellin' you there was somethin' grand about her, the way she talked in that quiet voice of hers that sometimes got shaky, she was that shy, and the way she looked at you with those big blue eyes as though she was jes trying to see inside of you and help you be good. I jes wanted to be near her and talk to her; and there was many a time when I was out tramping in these-here mountains with them hound dogs of mine and scouting for coon when I would jes sit down on some log and look over the valley on that-there mountain where she lived and wish I could be there and tell her how much I thought of her and how there was nothing in the world I would not do for her if she'd only let me. That's how much I cared for her.

Her parents were agin me. I couldn't blame them nohow. But I wasn't in love with them at that time. I was in love with Gracie, and we managed to steal meetings, and nobody but us knowed much about them nohow. There was a long winding lane between our homes. It was lined with big shady trees. And there was wild honeysuckle there. And, best of all, it sorter dipped out of sight between the two hills. It was sorter made for us to meet in. So of an evening Gracie would come along this way to get the cows for milking, and I most awful sudden found out there were a heap of squirrels along that old lane. So I would tote the old muzzle-loader and go hunting down that way. I don't recollect getting many squirrels. But I kinder used to always go back there every evening.

I was happy. I was happier than I had ever been before. You see I found love, too. When you have found that and peace of soul you are beginning to find out what life is all about. I guess them-there two things, love and peace, are what folks call the fundamental things.

The World War done broke out, but as you don't pay much attention nohow to a cloud when it first comes up in the sky, so I didn't pay none to the war. I scarcely heard or seed it. It didn't touch me. It didn't mean nothing to me. I knowed it was in Europe, but that moaned nothing to me. I knowed big nations were fighting, but I didn't know for sure how many and which ones. I didn't know what they were fighting for. I didn't know what it was all about. It was a long way from our peaceful little valley to them-there battlefields way across the sea. I read a little about it in the papers, and I heard them talking about it around the store. Not much, though, jes a little now and then.

So I went on with my farming and my church work and trying to court Gracie, when people were not around and I was lucky enough to meet her there in the lane. And I am a-telling you that kept me a-going. I had no time nohow to bother much about a lot of foreigners quarrelling and killing each other over there in Europe.

I had had fighting and quarrelling myself. I had found it bad. I had larned that it didn't profit a man nohow, and I had given it up forever, I hoped. I didn't want to go in for it again nohow. I jes wanted to be left alone to live in peace and love. I wasn't planning my life any other way. I didn't see that I had anything to do with them-there things away over in Europe. I kinder figured out that if some people were quarrelling and fighting in the valley next to ours it wasn't none of my business to go over there and interfere, and Europe was so much farther than any neighbouring valley. That's what the war meant to me.

I didn't think our country would get into it nohow. I didn't think we had anything to do with it. I never even dreamed that we would go over there and fight. Even when we got into it in 1917, it seemed a long way off and I didn't figure on being called. But the little cloud was growing blacker and bigger, and even in our little valley there was a heap more of this war talk. Some of the boys were talking of going away and fighting, and there was a tol'able lot of talk of the draft and of how we would all have to go. I couldn't see it that way. I couldn't sorter get interested, and I just didn't want to fight nohow.

I wasn't unpatriotic or disloyal or anything like that. I knowed my people for generations back had always fought for their country. I knowed we were all good Americans in the mountains, but that-there World War seemed such a long way off. So I didn't pay much attention to it. I didn't let it bother me.

I jes kept on a-going as I had been ever since I had been saved.

One summer afternoon I got my old squirrel gun and went down the lane as usual and met Gracie. I disremember what we talked about or how it happened, but I know we come to an understanding. I walked back home the happiest man that ever could be. I was kinder drunk with happiness. I had Gracie's promise that she would marry me. Her folks were agin me but she was for me. I sorter lived in a dream for the next few days. And then all of a sudden, out of nowhere, so it seemed to me, life sorter took me by the back of the neck and tried to lift me out of our little valley and throw me into the war over there in France. I received from the post office a little red card telling me to register for the draft.

I can't tell you how I felt. I just can't describe it. I was all mussed up. Everything was going from under me. Fight! Kill! And I'd been converted to the Gospel of peace and love, and of "Do good for evil."

That's how the war come to me, in the midst of all my peace and happiness and dreams, which I felt all along were too good to be true and just couldn't last.

CHAPTER 11

Conscientious Objector

In my records in the War Department in Washington, D. C., there is a little narrow pink slip, marked:

Conscientious Objector
YORK, ALVIN C.
Desires release as he is conscientious objector.
A. G- 383.2 Exemp Religious sects.
4-19-17-1918

So as long as the records remain I will be officially known as a conscientious objector. I was. I couldn't have been anything else nohow.

At first I jes couldn't imagine I would have to fight. The war seemed too far away to be mixing me up in it. And I didn't want to be in it nohow. I never had killed nobody, not even in my bad days, and I didn't want to begin now. I turned my back on all of those rowdy things and found a heap of comfort and happiness in religion. I joined the church. It was the Church of Christ in Christian Union. I had takened its creed and I had takened it without what you might call reservations. I was not a Sunday Christian. I believed in the Bible. And I tried in my own way to live up to it. It was the only creed of my church. To be a member I had to accept the Bible as the inspired word of God. I did. And the Bible said, "Thou shalt not kill." That was so definite a child could understand it. There was no way around or out of it. So you see there were two reasons why I didn't want to go to war. My own experience told me that it weren't right. And the Bible were agin it too.

But Uncle Sam said he wanted me and he wanted me most awful bad. And I had also been brought up to believe in my country. I knowed that even in the Civil War, when Tennessee was a doubtful state, my two grandfathers had both fought straight out for the Union. I knowed that, my great-great-grandfather, old Coonrod Pile, had been one of the pioneers who done helped to build up this-here country, and he hain't never hesitated to use a gun, and I kinder felt that my ancestors would want me to do whatever my country demanded of me.

So you see my religion and my own experience sorter told me not to go to war, and the memory of my ancestors jes as plainly sorter told me to get my gun and go and fight. I didn't know what to do. I am a-telling you there was a war going on inside of me and I didn't know which side to lean on. I was a heap bothered. Hit is a most awful thing when the wishes of your God and your country sorter get mixed up and go against each other. One moment I would make up my mind to follow God, and the next I would hesitate and almost make up my mind to follow Uncle Sam. Then I wouldn't know which to follow or what to do.

I wanted to follow both. But I couldn't. They were opposite. And I couldn't reconcile them nohow in my soul. I wanted to do what-was right. I wanted to be a good Christian and a good American too. I had always figured that the two were sort of connected. And now I was beginning to find out that they were kinder opposed to each other. If I went away to war and fought and killed, according to my reading of the Bible, I weren't a good Christian. And if I didn't go to war and do these things, according to Uncle Sam, I weren't a good American.

So I was the most bothered boy in all of these mountains. I didn't know what to do or where to turn. I walked the mountains night after night, trying to figure it out. I read the Bible over and over. I prayed and prayed, often late into the night. I got away off in the woods and I got out that little Government card telling me to register for the draft. I turned it over. I read and studied it. I jes couldn't make up my mind that the Bible were wrong. And I couldn't make up my mind Uncle Sam were right. I was a soul in doubt. I'm a-telling you, I was most unhappy.

Pastor Pile was the registrar. He had a store and the post office at Pall Mall, and the Government done instructed him to take the registration for the draft. I went to him and we talked it over, and we read the Bible and prayed together. No matter how we looked at it, we always come up against "Thou shalt not kill." That was the word of God and that was how it was revealed in His Holy Book. There was no gitting past that nohow.

So when I registered I claimed exemption from the draft. I wrote on the paper: "I don't want to fight." And that-there paper with that statement on it is now in the War Department in Washington, D. C.

A few weeks later I filed this application:

August 28, 1917

To LOCAL BOARD
COUNTY OF FENTRESS.

I, Alvin Cullum York, Serial Number 378, hereby certify that I am 29 years old and reside at Pall Mall, Tenn.

I hereby respectfully claim discharge from selective draft on the following ground, that I am—

(1) A person who was a member of a well recognized sect or organization, organized and existing May 18, 1917, whose then existing creed or principles forbade its members to participate in war in any form and whose religious principles are against war or participation therein in accordance with the creed or principles of said well recognized religious sect or organization.

But the Local Board refused to exempt me.

Local County Board of Fentress
STATE OF TENNESSEE, JAMESTOWN, TENN.

Serial No- 378

ALVIN CULLUM YORK Order No. 2 18

Denied, because we do not think "The Church of Christ in Christian Union" is a well-recognized religious sect, etc. Also, we understand it has no especial creed except the Bible, which its members more or less interpret for themselves, and some do not dis-believe in war-at least there is nothing forbidding them to participate.

Then I was bothered more than ever. I done done what I thought was right. I followed God, so I thought, even against the judgment of my country. I done wrote to the Board that I didn't want to go to war because I didn't want to kill; and because I belonged to a church which was opposed to war. And they done refused my appeal. But that didn't convince me nohow. I couldn't accept the written word of man against the written command of God. So I appealed against their decision. I wrote them:

LOCAL BOARD, FENTRESS COUNTY
STATE OF TENNESSEE
JAMESTOWN, TENN.
To LOCAL BOARD

I, Alvin Cullum York, Pall Mall, Tenn., now hereby claim an appeal to the District Board for Middle District of Tennessee, Nashville, Tenn., because you denied my claim for discharge which was based upon the ground that I am a member of a well-recognized religious sect or organization existing May 18, 1917, whose then existing creed or principles forbade its members to participate in war, etc.

A. C. YORK,
Pall Mall, Tenn.

And I also forwarded two affidavits, one from Pastor Pile and one from myself:

1. Affidavit of Person
Whose Discharge Is Sought.
State of Tennessee,
County of Fentress, to wit:

I, Alvin Cullum York, do solemnly affirm that I am 29 years old and reside at Pall Mall, Tenn., and that Serial Number 378 was given me by Local Board L. B. for County Fentress, and that claim for my discharge was filed with said Local Board on the 28th day of August, 1917, on the ground that I was a person who was a member of any well known religious organization, organized and existing May 18, 1917, whose then existing creed or principle forbade its members to participate in war in any form and whose religious principles are against war or participation therein, in accordance with the creed or principle of said religious organization.

I do further solemnly swear that I am a member, in good faith and good standing of the Church of Christ in Christian Union, which, on the 18th day of May, 1917, was organized and existing as a well recognized sect or organization whose existing creed or principles forbade its members to participate in war in any form.

I do further solemnly swear that my religious convictions are against war or participation therein in accordance with the creed or principles of said religious organization.

I do hereby bind myself to report in person and to notify said Local Board, at once, whenever the conditions entitling me to discharge cease to exist.

A. C. YORK,
Pall Mall, Tenn.

Subscribed and affirmed to before me this 1st day of Sept., 1917. Blaine Williams, Notary Public, State of Tennessee, County of Fentress.

2. Affidavit of Clerk of Minister in Support of Claim for Discharge.

State of Tennessee,
County of Fentress, to wit:

I, R. C. Pile, Minister, do solemnly affirm that I am the minister of the Church of Christ in Christian Union, and I hereby certify that A. C. York, who is personally known to me, is now a member of said religious sect or organization.

I do further solemnly affirm that the said religious sect or organization was organized and existing on the 18th day of May, 1917, and was then a well-recognized religious sect or organization, and that the then existing creed or principles of said religious sect or organization forbade its members to participate in war in any form.

I hereby bind myself that if the said person whose discharge is now sought ceases to be a member of said religious sect or organization, or if the existing creed or principles of said religious sect or organization are changed so as not to forbid its members participating in war in any form, or whenever the conditions entitling such person to discharge cease to exist I will at once notify said Local Board and will also request my successor in office to give such notice.

R. C. PILE,
Church of Christ in C. U.
Pall Mall.

I was now most awful worried. I was sorter mussed up inside worser'n ever. I thought that the word of God would prevail against all of the laws of man and of nations. I thought there must be some mistake somewhere. I knowed those words in the Holy Book come from God. I knowed He meant them and I knowed they must be right. I thought that I would not be a good Christian if I did not do all in my power to stick to them oncet I done accepted them. So I appealed to the Board again. I was sorter fighting against fighting. I mean I was fighting hard so I would not have to go to war and kill. It was sorter like a forest fire, when you fight fire with fire. I didn't understand it all. I only knowed I was troubled more'n I ever'd been before. I was up against the biggest thing I ever'd been up against. I'd used God's holy command in order to get an exemption from war. And now men who claimed they were jes as good Christians as I was, and were good churchmen too, although they didn't belong to my church, disallowed the words of God, as I had sent them in, and told me that I would have to go to camp and learn to fight and kill for my country. So I appealed again. So you see how I fought against going to war. I didn't hate nobody; I didn't want to kill nobody. I jes wanted to live and let live. I jes wanted to live my life in peace and I jes wanted to be let alone to love God and my fellowmen; and though the Germans were a long way off and I didn't know them, I figured jes the same they were my fellowmen. For the third time the Board refused to exempt me and wrote confirming their decision that I would have to go.

June 5, 1917

Pall Mall, Tennessee. Well, the first notice I receved was to go and register. So I did. And then I begun to think that I was going to be called to be examined.

I was lean and hard at that time. I'd been hunting, farming, blacksmithing, and driving steel. I had no fat on me at all. I was all bone and muscle. And I knowed I was, physically fit.

October 28, 1917

Jamestown, Tennessee. I was called to report to the Local Board for examination. So I went and when they look at me they weighted me and I weighted 170 lbs., was 72 inches tall. So they said I passed all right. Well, when they said that I almost knowed that I would haft to go to the army.

November 10, 1917

Pall Mall, Tennessee. So I just went on with my work and I receved a Little Blue Card that told me to be ready for a 24 hour call at any time.

I didn't pass judgment nohow on the members of the Board. I knowed it was written, "Judge not lest ye be judged." I was not even angry. I larned to kinder hold in my anger. I was only sad and sorry and bothered deep down in my soul. I thought that if I wanted to follow God and do His blessed will that was my own affair, and I would be left alone to do it. And I wanted to be left alone. I told them this again and again. I wrote it in my application. I swore it out in my affidavit, and they said jes the same I had to go I And worst of all, Pastor Pile, who was my friend and spiritual adviser, and who didn't want me to go any more'n I did want to go myself, had to be the one to register me. I often wondered why we have got to do things we don't want to do nohow, why, when we want to live in peace, we have to go away to war; why, when we say we are Christian nations, we don't try to live in peace and kinder respect people who love peace instead of sending them off to fight and kill, like they were going to send me.

And the worstest thing of all was that it was my country that was sending me. I'd always loved my country and believed in it. I was willing to live and work for it. If it wanted me to, I was willing to die for it. I hain't never been afraid to die, I am a-telling you. But my country wanted me to do more'n that; it wanted me to go and fight and kill others, and it said that it was right for me to do this, and God said it was not right. And there I was that way I didn't know what else to do but pray for the light. Then I received word to report to training camp.

November 14, 1917

Jamestown, Tennessee. So later I sure receved a card that said report to your Local Board. So I went to Jamestown, Tenn., and reported to the Local Board and I stayed all night that night with Doctor Alexander.

I knowed that I had to go. Of course, I could have run away and hid in the mountains, but I hain't never run away from anything before, except sin. I hain't never run away from my country. I hain't never done anything agin my country so I would have to run away. So I didn't. I could have stayed in Pall Mall and jes waited to see what happened, but then I knowed what would happen. The soldiers would come for me and takened me, and if I resisted there would be a fight, and maybe a killing, and that's jes what I didn't want to happen. I didn't want to fight or kill at home or anywhere else. So I reported.

CHAPTER 12

JOININ' UP WEREN'T NO PICNIC

November 15, 1917

Oneida, Tennessee. The morning of the 15th I started for the camp, which was Camp Gordon. I went to Oneida, Tenn., and stayed there until about 2 o'clock A.M. the next morning, when I entrained for Atlanta, Georgia.

I jes went to that old camp and said nothing. I did everything I was told to do. I never once disobeyed an order. I never once raised my voice in complaint, but I was sick at heart jes the same. I heard the boys around me talking about what fun it would be to go over seas and fight in the trenches. I heard them telling of how many Germans they were going to kill if ever they got a chance. I heard all sorts of things about the glory of war. But I couldn't see it like they seed it nohow. I prayed and prayed that God would show me His blessed will. And back there in the mountains Pastor Pile prayed and Mother prayed, too, and I jes knowed that all of those prayers would not be in vain. I jes knowed it

WAR

President Wilson's partial address to Congress
April 2, 1917

"It is a fearful thing to lead this great, peaceful country into war, into the most terrible and disastrous of all wars, civilization itself seeming to be in the balance. But the right is more precious than peace, and we shall fight for the things which we have always carried nearest our hearts—for democracy, for the right of those who submit to authority to have a voice in their own governments, for the rights and liberties of small nations, for a universal dominion of right by such a concert of free peoples as shall bring peace and safety to all nations and make the world itself at last free.

To such a task we can dedicate our lives and our fortunes, everything that we are and everything that we have, with the pride of those who know that the day has come when America is privileged to spend her blood and her might for the principles that gave her birth and happiness and the peace which she has treasured. God helping her, she can do no other."

—President Wilson to Congress, April 2, 1917.

Commander in Chief American Expeditionary Forces

"All instruction must contemplate the assumption of a vigorous offensive. This purpose will be emphasized in every phase of training until it becomes a settled habit of thought."

—General John J. Pershing

CHAPTER 13

Blessed are the Peacemakers

Facing the dangers of battle, many soldiers took their faith seriously, as did Alvin York.

I was detailed to Company G, 328th Division. That was a fighting division and was soon to be ordered overseas. I knowed that unless something happened I would have to go up into the front-line trenches and shoot and kill my brother men. I knowed that would be soon, too. And I didn't want to do that nohow.

So at last I went to my company commander, Captain Danforth, of Augusta, Ga., and I told him everything. I told him I belonged to a church that was opposed to war and that I didn't wish to be placed in a position that it might be necessary for me to kill a fellowman. I told him I hain't never talked about this in camp or disobeyed orders. I hain't never shirked my duty at no time. I hain't never refused to do anything he had ordered me to do, and I wasn't planning on refusing. I told him I knowed I was in the army and would have to obey. I would continue to be a soldier if I had to. I would go overseas. I would go in the front-line trenches. I would even kill Germans if I was ordered to. But I told him I wanted him to know I didn't believe in killing nohow, and that it worried me a-plenty. I told him all of this as man to man straight from the shoulder.

The Captain told me that there were several conscientious objectors in the camp, but that he sorter believed I was honest and sincere. I told him then how I had prayed and prayed. He assured me that he would consider everything I had told him and give me a right-square deal. A few days later he told me he done spoken to the battalion commander, Major Buxton, about me, and that the Major asked him if he believed I was sincere and when he said he believed I was, the Major done told him to bring me to his headquarters for questioning.

Major Buxton was from Providence, R. I. He was the first New Englander I ever knowed. He was a very good man, but at that time I was most troubled for his soul. I disliked to think that such a good man as he appeared to be would be willing to go to war and lead other men to fight. I couldn't understand how he could sorter square war and killing with his professed religious beliefs.

So one night Captain Danforth took me to Major Buxton's room to discuss these things with him. Before I done went I prayed to God for guidance. I took my Bible along with me. We all got together in his room there in Camp Gordon, which is in Georgia not far from Atlanta. The Major's room was like most of the officers' headquarters, jes a plain, small room. There was a little bed in it and some camp stools. There was a trunk in the corner and some military clothes hanging up or scattered around, and jes one light, a small electric light that hung down from the ceiling. The Major was very friendly-like; he always was with us boys. He told us to sit down. He said he didn't want to discuss this question as a battalion commander discussing it with an officer and a private. He wanted us to discuss it as three American citizens interested in a common cause. He said he respected any honest religious conviction and would be glad to discuss things as man to man. He asked me why was I opposed to going to war. I told him that I belonged to a church which disbelieved in fighting and killing. He then asked me what was the creed of the church. I told him the only creed was the Bible, and I also told him that I done accepted the Bible as the inspired word of God and the final authority for all men. So he then asked me what did I find in the Bible that was agin war, and I told him it was written, "Thou shalt not kill." He kinder looked at me for a moment and then asked if I accepted everything in the Bible, every sentence, every word, jes as completely as I accepted the Sixth Commandment, "Thou shalt not kill." I told him I did.

He then begun to read other parts of the Bible which he said proved that a man under certain conditions could go to war and fight and kill and still be a good Christian. He read a number of quotations. He read them well and accurate. I was kinder surprised at his knowledge of the Bible. It made me happy in my soul to know that my battalion commander was familiar with the word of God. I always thought Major Buxton was a good man, and now I knowed he was. Jes the same, he was for fightin'. I remember he begun by p'inting out that Christ once said: "He that hath no sword, let him sell his cloak and buy one." I 'lowed that was in the Bible. But I reminded him that Christ also said: "If a man smite you on one cheek, turn the other to him." He admitted that, but he asked me if I believed that the Christ who drove the money changers from the temple with the whip would stand up and do nothing when the helpless Belgian people was overrun and driven from their homes.

By this time we was at it right. We both knowed the Bible. I knowed now that I was on the right track. I knowed that if we studied the whole business through the words of the Lord, we must come to a right understanding. We talked along these lines for over an hour and every now and then Captain Danforth joined in. We didn't get annoyed or angry or even raise our voice. We jes examined the old Bible and whenever I would bring up a passage opposed to war, Major Buxton would bring up another which sorter favoured war. I believed the Lord was in that room. I seemed somehow to feel His presence there. I disremember a heap of what we said, but I know that I mentioned that when St. Peter struck off the ear of the high priest's servant, Christ, in restoring the ear, told Peter to put up the sword: "They that live by the sword shall die by the sword." But that-there Major Buxton knowed his Bible right smart. He come right back at me and answered that at the same time Christ also said: "For my kingdom is not of this world; but if my kingdom were of this world, then would my servants fight."

The Major then went on and said that the United States of America was an earthly government and its servants must fight for it whenever its liberties was threatened, and he reminded me that Christ said we must render unto Ceasar the things that are Ceasar's. And the Major 'lowed that Christ meant by this to emphasize the duties of Christians to their government. Major Buxton ended by quoting from Ezekiel:

"When I bring the sword upon a land, if the people of the land take a man of their coasts, and set him for their watchman:

If when he seeth the sword come upon the land, he blow the trumpet, and warn the people;

Then whosoever heareth the sound of the trumpet and taketh not warning, if the sword come and take him away, his blood shall be upon his own head.

He heard the sound of the trumpet, and he took not warning, his blood shall be upon him. But he that taketh warning shall deliver his soul.

But if the watchman see the sword come and blow not the trumpet, and the people be not warned, if the sword come and take any person from among them, he is taken away in his iniquity; but his blood will I require at the watchman's hands."

The Major made a great impression on me that night. A right-smart impression, too. He had kinder opened my eyes to things which were in the Bible, which I knowed were there, but which I hadn't thought of as he had thought of them. I ain't admitting that he had convinced me. He got me to thinking more and more. And more than ever now I didn't know what to do. I jes sat there and prayed and thought. He must have knowed it, too. He sorter looked at me and smiled, jes like my father used to. Then I told him that I would like time to think it over, and that in the meantime I would go on jes as I'd been, doing everything I was told to do and trying to be a good soldier. He shook hands with me and told me to take as long as I liked, and to come to him whenever I wished to. Then he said good-night, and Captain Danforth takened me back to my lines.

I spent considerable time turning the Major's arguments over in my mind that night and I worried and prayed 'most all through the night until reveille. The next morning I wrote in my little diary:

March, 1918

Camp Gordon, Georgia. Oh, these were trying hours for a boy like me, trying to live for God and do His blessed will, but yet I could look up and say:

> *O Master, let me walk with Thee, In lonely paths*
> *of service free, Tell me Thy secret, help me to bear,*
> *The strain of toil, the fret of care.*

And then the Lord would bless me and help me to bear my hard toiles.

But I couldn't get no understandin's around that-there old camp. I hain't been used to that. I sorter can't get alone with myself when there's crowds about. And I knowed I jes had to be alone to fight it out with myself. Hit was one of them-there sort of battles where nobody can help you nohow. You have jes got to help yourself. And I kinder knowed that the only place where I could do that was back there in the mountains where I belonged. There's heaps of peace there. I jes knowed I had to go back, or else I would always be sorter twistin' in torment like them-there lost souls that can't never see the light nohow. So I applied for leave and I was given a pass for ten days.

March 21-31, 1918

Pall Mall, Tennessee. So I got a pass after a while for 10 days. So I went home and while I was at home we had several services at Greer's Chaple, and the Lord blessed us and we had a fine meeting. Rev. R. C. Pile and others were helping, and there were a number of people saved during this little meeting. So the Lord was with us. Bless His holy name.

I knowed now that if I went back and told the Major I was still opposed to fighting he would let me out or have me transferred into another branch of the service where I wouldn't have to kill. He knowed now that I was sincere. He was a good man. He would help me. But something in me had kinder changed. I was beginning to see war in a different light. I had takened to heart and read over and over again them-there passages from the Bible he had read to me. I kinder balanced them against the passages that made me a conscientious objector. I had tried to bring the two together. I knowed the *"Lord worked in marvellous ways, His wonders to perform."* I knowed that He had His own way of saying and doing things. I knowed that if it was His will He would even use war as an instrument in His hands. I tried to look at it this way. I talked to Pastor Pile again and again. But all I got from all of this was to get more and more confused than ever. I jes didn't know what to do; whether to want war or peace; and I didn't know which He wanted me to do.

So I went out on the mountainside and asked Him sorter straight out from the shoulder. I went off to a quiet place not far from my home. I knelt down and I prayed and I prayed all the afternoon, through the night and through part of the next day. I asked Him to have pity on me and show me the light. I begged

Him to comfort me if it was His will and tell me what to do. And as I prayed there alone a great peace kinder come into my soul and a great calm come over me and I received my assurance. He heard my prayer and He come to me on the mountainside. I didn't see Him, of course, but He was there jes the same. I knowed He was there. He understood that I didn't want to be a fighter or a killin' man, that I didn't want to go to war and hurt nobody nohow. And yet I wanted to do what my country wanted me to do. I wanted to serve God and my country, too. He understood all of this. He seed right inside of me, and He knowed I had been troubled and worried, not because I was afraid, but because I put Him first, even before my country, and I only wanted to do that which would please Him.

So He took pity on me and He gave me the assurance I needed. I didn't understand everything. I didn't understand how He could let me go to war and even kill and yet not hold it agin me. I didn't even want to understand. It was His will and that was enough for me. So at last I begun to see the light. I begun to understand that no matter what a man is forced to do, so long as he is right in his own soul he remains a righteous man. I knowed I would go to war. I knowed I would be protected from all harm, and that so long as I believed in Him He would not allow even a hair of my head to be harmed.

I arose and thanked Him and went home over the mountains, singing a hymn.

I told my little old mother I was going and not to worry. I was coming back safe and sound. I told my brothers and sisters and I told Pastor Pile. And for a while I was happy and at peace with myself and with my God.

But when I went back to camp and seed all the boys there getting ready to go to the war, some of the old worries come a-piling back on my soul. I knowed I was all right. But I kinder got a-figurin' that the whole thing was a heap bigger than my own personal peace of soul. I might be safe myself, but in going over there and fightin' I might be helping to have them killed and a heap more of others, too, and that worried me.

I knowed He was going to watch over me, because I done done what I thought was right. But I wanted Him to watch over all of us, and I knowed He would only do that if we were all right and if our cause was right, too. I kinder felt now that it was right. But I wasn't sure. It's most awful hard for a weak human being, all sort of torn up with doubt and worry, to walk his way in perfect faith and understanding.

Pastor Pile wrote direct to President Wilson and explained things to him and asked him to release me. The letter come on down to our camp in Georgia. But I didn't follow it up. I didn't make any more claims for exemption. I didn't try to get out nohow. I knowed I was to go, but— was still worrying about the war in general.

We moved up to Camp Upton, N. Y., and prepared ourselves to go overseas. So I went to the Captain again, Captain Danforth of Augusta, Ga., and asked him to please explain to me what we were fighting for and why we were leaving our homes and going over there to fight people we didn't even know and had never met before. The Captain kinder looked at me, funny like, as though he had thought he had settled all of that with me once before. But jes the same he was patient. Lieutenant Stewart, who, later on, was killed in the Argonne, was there in the orderly room with him and he was patient, too. They explained to me how the Germans done broken their promise to Belgium and done overrun those countries over there and put so many people to the sword; that unless they were stopped they would keep on until they done overrun the world. They jes had to be stopped and we Americans were going over there to help stop them.

Then I begun to understand, not clearly yet, but kinder like.

We were to be peacemakers. And it was written in the Bible, *"Blessed are the peacemakers."*

That was we-uns. We were to help make peace, the only way the Germans would understand. But I couldn't help a-wonderin' why there wasn't some other way to get peace except by fightin' for it.

CHAPTER 14

Background to Lost Ground

Archduke Francis Ferdinand (heir to the Austrian throne) with his wife. Both were assassinated at Sarajevo, Bosnia, June 28, 1914. This was the trigger that started WWI.

In 1914, a small Austrian province called Bosnia provided the fuse to set off the touchy explosive European aggression that led to World War I . Bosnia bordered the Serbian state, which had won its independence from the Turks in the 1840s and was still aggressively seeking territory. Because Bosnia had a large population of ethnic Serbs, many Austrians feared that Serbia would attack Austria and try to annex Bosnia. The Austrians felt their neighbors needed to be taught a lesson—especially once the world learned of the Black Hand, an organization formed in 1911 to win Serbian unity through acts of terrorism. Between January 1913 and June 1914, the Austrian army chief of staff recommended going to war with Serbia on 25 occasions. In the summer of 1914, as a show of strength, Austria sent 70,000 troops on military maneuvers to Bosnia.

On June 28, 1914, Archduke Franz Ferdinand, heir to the throne of Austria-Hungary, went to the Bosnian capital of Sarajevo to review the Austrian troops stationed there; his wife, Sophie, accompanied him. Austrian spies in Serbia had warned of a possible assassination attempt, but the trip was not postponed. As their motorcade made its way down Sarajevo's main street, 120 policemen guarded the route and six young Serbian men, holding guns and bombs supplied by the Black Hand, waited to try to kill the archduke.

Franz Ferdinand's car passed two conspirators without incident. But then the car passed the third conspirator, Cabrinovic, who threw a bomb. The bomb bounced off the back of the archduke's car and blew up the car behind. Alerted to danger, the motorcade sped away to the town hall. Frustrated over their foiled opportunity, the conspirators were about to abandon their plans.

At the town hall, the archduke decided to cancel his visit and return by a different route. Confused about the new plan, the archduke's driver made a wrong turn onto a narrow side road. General Potiorek, the governor of Bosnia, who was riding in the car with the royal couple, shouted to the driver to reverse. But as the archduke's car backed up slowly, a fourth conspirator, Gavrilo Princip, appeared, drew his revolver, and fired. The first shot hit Franz Ferdinand in the neck, A second, aimed at Potiorek, hit Sophie in the stomach. Within moments, Franz Ferdinand and Sophie were dead.

The Serbian terrorists had achieved their goal, but the consequences of the murders would reach far beyond Bosnia, Serbia, and Austria-Hungary. "If I had foreseen what was to happen," said Cabrinovic later, "I should have sat down on the bombs and blown myself to bits."

GERMAN EMPEROR WILHELM II ABDICATED NOVEMBER 28, 1918

Franz Ferdinand's murder outraged Kaiser Wilhelm of Germany. He was all too eager to see Germany assume its "place in the sun," and he feared that the assassination would weaken Germany's ally, Austria-Hungary, and might even bring that empire to the verge of collapse. "Now or never... it is high time a clean sweep was made of the Serbs," he wrote on June 30, 1914. Kaiser Wilhelm found support among the German army commanders. "We are ready, and the sooner the better for us," said General Helmuth von Moltke, who claimed that war offered "the last means of preserving Austria-Hungary."

On July 5, therefore, Wilhelm assured the Austrian government that it could "in this case, as in all others, rely on

Germany's full support." The next day, he referred to the Agadir crisis of 1911 when he told a friend, "This time I won't chicken out."

On July 23, the Austrian government sent the Serbian government a forcefully worded ten-point ultimatum requiring it to stamp out all opposition to Austria-Hungary. Point Six demanded an inquiry into Franz Ferdinand's assassination, at which Austrian delegates were to be present and active. The Austrian government intended that the terms of this ultimatum would be impossible to accept. Because Serbia would lose its rights of government if it agreed to all of Austria demands, the Serbs would surely reject the ultimatum; in this way, Austria would appear justified in declaring war. To make any diplomatic solution to the crisis more difficult, Serbia was given a mere 48 hours to reply.

Russia, alarmed at the growth of Austrian power in the Balkans, sent the Serbs a strong letter of support. Despite this offer, the Serbian government tried to avoid a conflict. They responded quickly and accepted all the Austrian demands except Point Six, which went against Serbian law.

The Austrian government, however, was not interested in compromise; it wanted blood and vengeance for the assassination of their archduke. On July 28, 1914, it sent a telegram to Serbia, declaring war. Later that day, Austrian guns began to bombard the Serbian capital, Belgrade.

For two days, the Russian government debated how to respond. Few Russians wanted war. Russia, however, had promised to support the Serbs; to let the Austrians destroy Serbia would damage Russia's prestige. The last Czar of Russia, Nicholas II, was at first uncertain what to do. However, on July 31, determined to act decisively, he ordered his army commanders to prepare for action and mobilize the troops.

CHAPTER 15

"I'M IN THE ARMY NOW, NOT BEHIND A PLOW"

And all of this time while I was struggling with my doubts I was going on with my training and sorter fitting into camp life. I obeyed orders. I did everything I was told to do. I tried my best to be a good soldier.

November, 1917

Camp Gordon, Georgia. I was placed in the 21st Training Bn. 82 Division, and there I was called out the first morning of my army life to police up in the yard all the cigarette buts, and I thought that was pretty hard as I didn't smoke but I did it just the same.

I hain't never travelled much before going to camp. I hain't never been out of the mountains before, and I'm a-telling you I missed them right smart. It's pretty flat and sandy country down there in Georgia, and there ain't no strength or seasonin' in it. Hit shore needs hills and mountains most awful bad.

December, 1917

Camp Gordon, Georgia. So I stayed there and did squads right and squads left until the first of February, 1918, and then I was sent to Company G 328 Bn-82 Div.

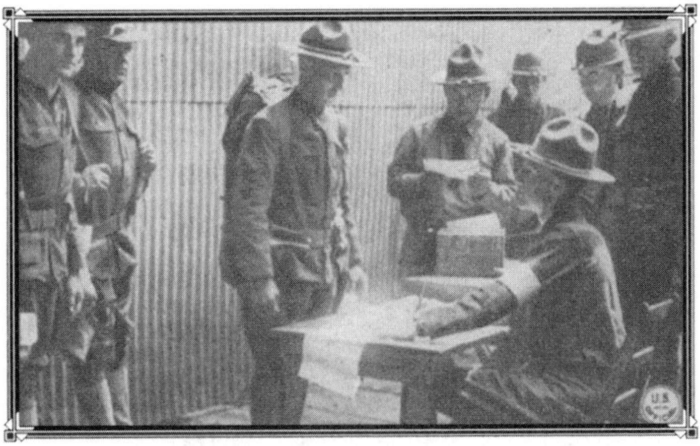

Camp life was pretty dull at first. York was real homesick.

All that the new recruits did the first few days was hike all the time.

CHAPTER 16

THE ALL-AMERICAN

EIGHTY-SECOND DIVISION

The Eighty-second Division was known as the All-American Division. We wore the insignia A A on our shoulder. We were made up of boys from most every state in the Union. There were some mountaineers. Not many of them, though. Jes a few. There were Jews from the East Side of New York; there were English and Irish boys from the mill towns of New England; there were Greeks and Italians from some of the big cities in the East; there were Poles and Slavs from the coal mines of Pennsylvania; there were farmers from the Middle West; there were cow punchers from Oklahoma and Texas; and there were even some German boys. One-fifth of our men were of foreign birth, and several hundred were not even citizens of the United States. A right-smart number of them couldn't speak or understand the American language. And a whole heap couldn't read or write or even sign their own name.

February, 1918

Camp Gordon, Georgia. So there they put me by some Greeks and Italians to sleep. Well, I couldn't understand them and they couldn't understand me, and I was the homesickess boy you ever seen, ho ! ho !

I had never had nothing to do nohow with foreigners before. When I first heard them talk I kinder thought they were angry with each other they seemed to talk so fast and loud. I couldn't pronounce their names nohow. There was a great big Pole in our outfit whose name was Private Feodor Sok. That was easy. We jes called him Sok. There was another, Private Maryan E. Dymowski. I never could get the straight of that nohow. And then there was Private Joe Konotski. I couldn't do much with that either. And there was Private Mario Muzzi and Michael Saccina. These are only a few of the foreigners we done had in my platoon. But they kinder give some idea of what a mixed-up gang we had in the All-American Division.

Our battalion commander was Major George Edward Buxton, Jr., from Providence, R. I. He was a New Englander. His beginnings went away back; so far back that I guess he can scarcely trace them himself. He was one of the finest men I had ever met. He was one of the most larned men too; and he was a right-smart mixer. He was one of the best soldiers I ever knowed. Before America come into the war he was over there on the other side writing for the Providence, R. I., Journal. When he returned home he jes knowed America was coming in, so he got busy doing everything he could to prepare us for when our turn came. He takened part in the Preparedness Campaign with ex-President Roosevelt. He went to Plattsburg and he was one of the first officers to be commissioned there. He went all over the country preaching preparedness.

He was a most wonderful man at handling soldiers. He had a battalion mixed up of all sorts. And yet he knowed most all of us and understood us and figured out the way to handle us. He was young for a commanding officer, in his early thirties, I reckon. He was handsome, and in his major's uniform he looked a right-smart soldier. He had a kinder habit of getting us soldiers together and talking to us, something like a father talks to his sons. I'm a-tellin' you he sorter looked upon us as his sons, too. And in quicker time than it takes a coon to jump out of a tree he made that torn-up battalion all around us into a happy family.

I ricollect a heap of our fellows were sorter short on this saluting business. So one day the Major got us together and talked to us. He told us that we were soldiers and we had to salute. Then he explained to us that when we saluted an officer we weren't admittin' nohow that we were under him or inferior to him; we were jes letting him know that we were his friends. He told us how the salute began. It was over there in England. They had a big Civil War something like ours here in America. The side that was beaten was mussed up awful bad. Some of them were killed. Some of them were put in jail. Some of them were shipped away acrost the seas. And a whole heap of them were driven into the forest where they were hunted jes like wild animals. They had to keep moving jes in order to keep alive. Their sufferings sorter drew them together. Of course, they were desperate and did a lot of killing. But not among themselves. Whenever they come together in the forest they would hold out their right hand to show they didn't have a gun in it and that they were friendly. That was the beginning of it, so the Major explained to us. And after a while it was sorter takened up by the English army and made over into the salute. And so Major Buxton pointed out that if we didn't salute him and his officers he would take it that we were not friendly, and if the officers didn't salute us back we were to take it that way.

After that there was no more trouble about this saluting business. Our boys were so friendly they would salute every chance they got, and the Major had to sorter slow us down. I ricollect another little talk he gave us. He said in every war there was always one famous battalion that come out of it and sorter lived forever. He hoped that battalion would be ours. And every war always produced its outstanding hero. He didn't know where that hero was in the American Army, but there was jes as good a chance of him being in our battalion as anywhere else. And I'm a-tellin' you after we heard him speak like that we all kinder made up our minds to be better soldiers and maybe try and be that outstanding one ourselves. His favourite advice to us was "Keep moving and always use your head." I'm saying here and now that's right-smart advice.

Captain E. C. B. Danforth, Jr., was my company commander. He come from Augusta, and was a Georgia "Cracker." He was a Harvard man. That didn't mean nothing to me in those days. It didn't mean much to the other boys either. All we knowed was that like the Major he had a heap of larnin'. He was tall and tough jes like a hickory pole. He must have been about twenty-three or twenty-four years old, and he had as much sense as a much older man. He was the fightinest man, too, and when he was in action our boys used to say he was that hard that the bullets used to bounce off'n him. The Major and the Captain together were as good a combination as a pair of Red Bones when you have them out after the foxes. They ran together. If ever I have to go to war agin I'm a-telling you I wouldn't ask for anything more than to have them two leading me. Wherever they go I am willing to follow. And that's jes about how most of the other boys under them feel.

My own platoon was made up of a gang of the toughest and most hard-boiled doughboys I ever heard tell of. There were bartenders, saloon bouncers, ice men, coal miners, dirt farmers, actors, mill hands, and city boys who had growed up in the back alleys and learned to scrap ever since they were knee high to a duck. They were mixed up from 'most every country. They were as hard as a forest full of oaks and they were meaner and more full of fight than a hive of wild bees. They could outswear, out-drink, and out-cuss any other crowd of men I have ever knowed. They sorter looked upon leave-breaking as a divine right.

Our sergeant takened forty-eight hours' leave and stayed away ten days. He was busted for that, but later on he got his stripes back. He had to. He was the only one who could drill and keep us in hand. One of our corporals went on leave and missed the boat and had to follow us to France.

They were always spoiling to have it out with somebody. They were fighters and that's all about it. If you looked at them sorter sideways for even a second you were in danger of being on the wrong end of a punch. If you didn't drink they kinder regarded you as being ignorant; and if you didn't cuss a blue streak every time you opened your mouth you were considered to be most awful illiterate.

A heap of them couldn't talk our own language at all, and any number of them couldn't sign their own names. The only way the Captain could get them to larn to write was by telling them they couldn't get their pay unless they could put their signatures to the pay sheets. Ho! Ho!

But jes the same, they were my buddies. I didn't understand them at first. I didn't know nothing about them nohow. I didn't cuss or drink or smoke or fight. I didn't go A. W. 0. L. [absence without official leave]. And I was a conscientious objector. So they didn't understand me either. But most they left me alone. And that's all that I asked for. So they let it go at that.

I guess Major Buxton and Captain Danforth must have lost a heap of sleep trying to figure out how to handle that-there gang of wild men. But I'm a-thinking them-there officers knowed in their hearts that if ever they got them safe overseas and into the front-line trenches they would have a bunch of fighters under them that never would stop until they done mussed up the Germans right smart and busted a hole right through that-there old Hindenburg Line. But the puzzling thing was to keep them together and to handle them in the right sort of way until they were overseas. That was a job, I'm a-tellin' you, and I ain't a-foolin' nohow. Them-there boys jes had to fight.

The sergeant in charge of our platoon was Harry Parsons, of Brooklyn, N. Y. He'd been an actor and he was jes a natcheral-born entertainer. He used to lead us in singing. He used to entertain us at night, and when we were out on a long route march and were tired out he would gather us around and go to it and then we would all get to laughing and singing. That's one of the ways he handled us. He was a big husky sort of fellow. He knowed how to handle that platoon. He didn't fight unless he had to, and then he had a habit of biting his teeth together and putting his chin out and letting fly with both hands at the same time. And when he did that somebody went down, and it was never him. But he never manhandled our fellows unless he had to. But when he had to he made a right-smart job of it. Something must have happened to him over there in the Argonne, because when he come home he was changed. He went back on the stage but he done lost his power to entertain.

Then we had two of the wildest fighting corporals that ever knocked them down and dragged them out. One of them was Bernard Early. He used to be a bartender in Connecticut. The amount of liquor he could put away was most amazing. And when it come to fighting he jes couldn't be beat. Early come from Ireland where they jes natcherly breed fighting men. In and around the camp, in the saloon or over in the front lines in France, it was all the same to Bernie. If there was a fight he was happy. If there wasn't he was kinder always looking for one. But he was a friendly chap, and he had a sorter way with him. He was a right-smart soldier, too, most awful brave. I guess he hain't never known what fear was.

His particular buddy was another corporal, William S. Cutting. He was a Pole from around Boston and New York, where he used to be an ice man. He was always rarin' to go. You ought to've heard him talk. He was funny-oncet he said that when he got into the front-line trenches if the Germans ever threw bombs at him he would jes eat them-there bombs for breakfast. These-here two corporals were jes about the hard-boiledest soldiers I ever knowed. It took me a long time to understand them, and I'm a-thinkin' I ain't never really done it. But jes the same, once they done gone into action, they shore enough cost the Germans a heap more bother than a whole swarm of hornets or bumblebees ever could have.

Among the privates was that-there Sok. For a long time I didn't even know that was his real name. I thought it was a nickname. When he went berserker over there at the front it looked as if he never would stop nohow until he got right through to Berlin.

Then there was Michael Saccina, a little Italian. I think he come from New York. After the fight in the Argonne he likened the German Major's whistle to the little whistle on a peanut stand at home in New York. That sorter speaks for itself.

And there was Joe Konotski and Walter Swanson and Muzzi and Beardsley and Johnson and a heap of others; all of them most awful hard fightin' men and most awful tough soldiers. Most of them were always causing a lot of trouble; but they bothered the Germans a heap more than they bothered anybody else. I ricollect, too, we had a couple of farm boys from the South with us. Ho! ho! When we were in New York, before sailing, they got their safety razors. They didn't understand them nohow. One of them fixed up his razor and tried to shave with it, but it weren't no good. He looked at it and said: "Anything the Government gives you for nothing ain't never no good," and with a sort of disgusted look on his face he throwed it away. The other one tried several times without even cutting a hair. Then he throwed his away too, and said he "never had no use for the Democrats nohow," and now they were in power they had to go and buy razors that wouldn't shave. Ho! Ho! They were trying to shave with the wax paper on the blades !

So these were the sort of soldier boys that I was in with in the Eighty-second Division. Jes a bunch of hard-living, hard-fighting doughboys; always spoiling for a scrap. But when you got to know them, they were jes about as fine a bunch of buddies as ever got together and did squads right and squads left, and when they got into it over there they jes kept on a-goin'.

Of course, it takened me a long time to get to know them. In camp I never did think I would larn to understand them, and I guess they couldn't figure me out nohow. They knowed that I was a conscientious objector, and they hadn't much use for that. They jes didn't understand. Sometimes they got to teasing me most awful bad, but I never done any arguing with them. I hadn't anything to say or any fault to find, and I wasn't going to quarrel or fight with them no matter what they done. I didn't want to fight nobody and least of all American doughboys. So we went on training together through the early months of 1918.

CAMP TRAINING

Jumping into the "enemy's" trench with fixed bayonets.

"Going over the top."

Bayonet practice with simulated war conditions
while wearing gas masks and "tin hats."

Grenade throwing

Machine gun instruction

CHAPTER 17

SHOOTIN' THE BREEZE

March, 1918

Camp Gordon, Georgia. Well, they give me a gun and oh my that old gun was jes full of Greece and I hed to clean that old gun for enspection. So I had a hard time to get that old gun clean. So when I got this gun I begin to drill with the gun, and we had to hike once a week. So I have seen many boys fall out of the hikes. We would haft to take long hikes with all our stuff on our back and carry that gun. Ho! Ho! And we would haft to go out before daylight and have sham battles.

That first army rifle that was issued me was all full of grease, gun grease of some kind. Of course, I didn't like that. The rifles we used in the mountains 'we always kept clean. They were most all muzzleloaders. And I'm a-tellin' you up to one hundred yards they could out-shoot them-there army rifles anytime. But, of course, a muzzle-loader wouldn't be no good nohow in a modern war. It takes too long to reload. It don't carry far enough, and it's too heavy. So I had to get used to the army rifle. And I did. I cleaned it up. I takened it to pieces. I put it together agin. I nursed it and doctored it. It larned all about it.

Then we went out on the rifle ranges to practise shooting. Them-there Greeks and Italians and Poles and New York Jews and some of the boys from the big cities hadn't been used to handling guns. Some of them didn't even know how to load them, and when they fired they not only missed the targets, they missed the backgrounds on which the targets were fixed. They missed everything but the sky. It shore was dangerous scoring for them boys. Of course, it weren't no trouble nohow for me to hit them great big army targets. They were so much bigger than turkeys' heads. And an army bull's-eye is about a million times bigger than a criss-cross cut with a sharp knife on a piece of board or a tree; and that's the target we most often used in our shooting matches at home. We had to cut the centre right out to win anything. That's the sort of shooting I was used to. So I made a tol'able score on the shooting ranges in camp.

York astounded the field trainers with his shooting ability. He shot so well that they commissioned him to train the men in his division.

York could shoot with a pistol as well as with a rifle. The rifle, a 30-06 Eddystone, and 45 cal pistol were new compared to his primitive style single-shot muzzle loader. However, he soon gained mastery over them, saving his life, as well as the lives of many of his unit.

March 20, 1918

So I begin to want a pass to go home and applied for a pass which was given to me. I takened the train as far as I could and then I hiked the last twelve miles over the mountains, alone. I had to carry my suit case, too. Ho! Ho!

York to leave and returned to his beloved valley, family, and friends, and future wife, Gracie.

It kinder hurt to say good-bye to Mother. And I jes knowed I would never forget that-there last meeting in the lane with Gracie. But I ain't a-writing about those things. There are some things in your life that you can't do nothing else with but jes sorter feel deep inside of you. And that's the way it was with me.

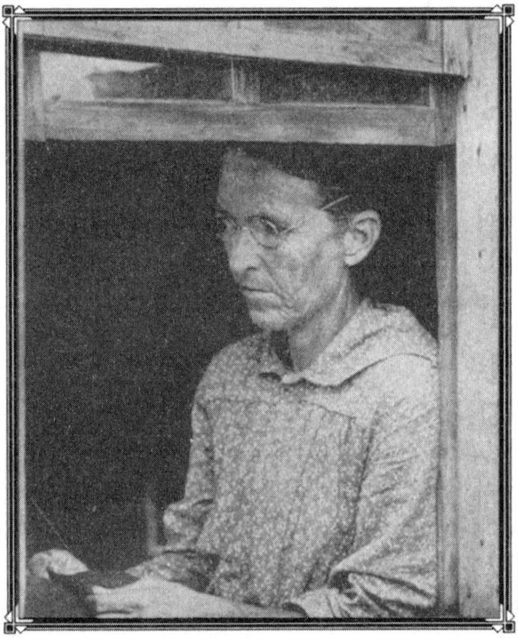

York was very close to his mother, Mary.
She raised him to be God-fearing,
honest, and hard-working.

March 29, 1918

Pall Mall, Tennessee. So I had to start back to my company, and that was a heart-breaking time for me, as I knowed I had to go to France. But I went back to my company, trusting in my God and asking Him to keep me, although I had many trials and much hardship and temptation. But yet I could look up and say:

"O God, in hope that sends the shining ray, Far down the future's broadening way; In peace that only Thou canst give; With Thee, O Master, let me live."

Then it was that the Lord would bless me, and I almost felt sure of coming back home, for the Lord was with me.

April 19, 1918

Camp Gordon, Georgia. So we left Camp Gordon in the afternoon.

April 21, 1918

Camp Upton, New York. We got to Camp Upton, New York, so we stayed there a few days and drilled.

Arriving in New York was a fearful experience for Alvin. The "county boy" in him never left, and cities never had an appeal to him.

CHAPTER 18

THE YANKS ARE A-COMIN'

Troops being transported overseas.

Editor's note:

During our 19 months of involvement in the war, more than 2,000,000 American soldiers were carried to France. Half-a-million of these went over in the first 13 months and one million and a half in the last 6 months.

The highest troop-carrying records are those of July, 1918, when 306,000 soldiers were carried to Europe and May, 1919, when 330,000 were brought home to America.

Most of the troops who sailed for France left from New York. Half of them landed in Great Britain and the other half landed in France.

Among every 100 Americans who went overseas, 49 went in British ships, 45 in American ships, 3 in Italian, 2 in French, and 1 in Russian shipping under English control.

Our cargo ships averaged one complete trip every 70 days and our troop ships one complete trip every 35 days.

The cargo fleet was almost exclusively American. It reached 2,600,000 tons (dead weight) to Europe.The greatest troop-carrier among all the ships has [[landed 12,000 men, or the equivalent of a German division, in France every month.

The fastest transports have been the Great Northern and the Pacific, which have made complete turnarounds, taken on and started back again in 19 days.

York continues his narrative:

May, 1918

Boston, Mass. About 4 o clock am we got on board the old Scandaneven ship and started for France.

Left Boston and sailed down around to New York Harbour and we stopped there until we got our convoy, and then we lit out. And that was the first time that I had ever seed the open sea. It was too much water for me. Like me, Mark Twain, whose parents come from Jimtown, was borned inland. And he never seed the open ocean until he growed up. And when he stood on the beach and seed it for the first time, his friends asked him what he thought of it, and he said, "It was a success." But when Mark said that he weren't on the ocean. He were on the shore. And when our old boat got away out and begun to pitch and toss I jes knowed Mark was wrong.

The Greeks, Italians, and Poles, and New York Jews stood the trip right smart. That kinder impressed me. It sorter made up for their bad shooting. I sorter got to like them more.

May 16

Liverpool, England. We got off the boat in the evening.

May 17

Camp Knotteash, England. We stayed at a little camp called Knotteash on the 17th.

May 18

Southampton, England.

May 20

Southampton, England.

We started from England to France.

So you see I didn't see much of England. I'd travelled over three thousand miles from my home to get there, and when I did get there all I did was hike and catch trains and keep moving. I might jes as well have been in Georgia, only the English country was more beautiful. It was sort of rolling-like and the parksand fields were so neat and tidy that it 'most looked as though they had special gardeners to look after every few acres of them.

Of course, we were all anxious to get to France. We wanted to get into it and get it over. We had a sorter idea that they would rush us right to those old front-line trenches and let us get at the Germans without losing any time.

Anxious to get to France.

May 21, 1918

Le Havre, France.

So we got to France at Le Havre where we turned in our guns and got British guns. (Americans were issued 303 British

Enfields in order to keep ammunition uniform)

We crossed the English Channel on the H. M. S. Viper. It was more like a bucking mule than a boat. We were only on it for a few hours, but that was a-plenty. Long before we landed I didn't care whether we stayed up or went down, whether we got there or didn't get there. I didn't care about anything. I was kinder miserable. I missed the mountains of Tennessee morein ever.

French celebrate the arrival of the Americans.

We spent our first night in France in a little camp outside of Le Havre. We had to turn in our guns and get British guns. I had takened a liking to mine by this time. I had takened it apart and cleaned it up so often that I had learned every piece and could almost put it back together with my eyes shut. The Greeks and Italians and Jews and Poles were improving. They had stayed continuously on the rifle range for a month or two, and got so they could do shooting. They were fairly good pals, too. But I missed the mountain boys. I was the only mountaineer in the company. I was the largest in our platoon.

Alvin York wrote:
"We got our first gas masks in Le Havre, France.
That brought the war a whole heap closer.
I never did like those pesky gas masks."

"We travelled in box cars. They were marked,
"Forty men or eight horses." One of our boys who was
detailed to load the cars went to the Captain and said:
"Captain, I loaded the forty men all right, but if you put
the eight horses in too they will shore trample
the boys to death." Ho! ho!

CHAPTER 19

THE ALLIES

Field Marshal Douglas Haig,
Commander in Chief
of the British armies in France.

May 22-24th

Taken the train at Le Havre, France and come to a little place called Eu. We eat our Breakfast at Eu and then Hiked to Floraville, and we stayed at floraville a few days.

Field Marshal Haig and his staff inspected one of our battalions here. The British commander made a right-smart impression on the boys. While he was with them he went and inspected one of the kitchens. One of the cooks was a great big fellow from Tennessee, and the Field Marshal asked him if everything was all right, and he said, "No, everything is all wrong, most awfully all wrong—there is no salt." The Field Marshal turned to the Quartermaster General, who was with him, and asked for an explanation. The Quartermaster said the two last salt ships were torpedoed and there was a shortage. The Field Marshal then instructed him to immediately send some salt to the American kitchen. That kinder tickled our boys.

Our own General Pershing also inspected us. We were anxious to make a right-smart impression on him, because we knowed if we did we would get up to the front-line trenches so much quicker, and our boys were jes rarin' to go. General Pershing made even a better impression than Field Marshal Haig, and he seemed sorter satisfied with us. So you see here we were in France. And we were inspected by two commanders-in-chief and we got by all right. We shore were a different outfit to the rambunshus crowd of half-wild men that first got together in Camp Gordon, in Georgia.

Anyone who thinks that soldiering is jes goin' back in again and fightin', is jes plumb foolin' himself. Weeks passed and we never even seen a trench except the training ones. We never once heard the sound of guns. All we did was hike, and hike, and hike-and then hike again. They shore kept us a-going-hiking. It seemed as though they had sent us to France to kinder test out the strength of them-there American military shoes.

June 4

Mons Babert, France.

Hiked here and we stayed a few Days. And the boys were beginning to think by this time that we weren't a-fightin' outfit at all. We were jes sorter touring France-on the hoof. Ho! Ho! I didn't mind it much because I was used to hunting and tramping over the mountains. But them-there Greeks and Jews and Italians from the cities shore filled their shoes full of blisters. But they kept a-going jes the same. I'm a-tellin' you them boys were coming along right smart. I was beginning to get kinder fond of them. They were sorter human jes like the mountain boys I had knowed all my life. Of course, they were not as strong or as good hikers or shooters, but I was beginning to larn they had a few things about them which the mountain boys didn't have nohow. Them there city boys shore nursed their feet, jes about as careful as I nursed my guns.

York did not like the party life of the soldier who spent time off drinking and meeting French women. He would stay at camp, read the Bible, and write in his diary.

Of course, of a night time if we was near a town, some of the boys got leave. Some of them got all tanked up with vin rouge and cognac; and, being soldiers, they was right smart when it come to finding them-there pretty French girls. Some of them shore knowed more about hunting and finding them, too, than I did about trailing coon and fox back there on the mountains at home. They were fuller of fight than ever. It was in them and it had to come out. They couldn't get at the Germans yet, so they sorter practised out on themselves. There was a heap of Irish and Poles in our platoon, and one night in one of the cafe's one of the Irish boys said he didn't believe the Poles could fight nohow. Ho! Ho! That shore started it! They went at it with fists and belts. They turned that cafe into a No Man's Land, only worse, and we had to turn out the guard to stop it. I'm a-tellin' you there was nothin' mean or bad about the boys. They was jes sorter full of life.

I didn't go into the towns much. I had put all of the drinkin' and fist-fightin' away behind me. I left it back home on the Kentucky line. I didn't have a drink all the time I was in France.

I didn't have a fist fight or an argument. I didn't swear or smoke either. I wasn't any better'n any of the other boys. It was jes my way of livin', that was all. They did what they wanted to do. So did I. Our ways were different. We let it go at that. I did a heap of reading from the Bible. I read it through several times over there. I worked on my little diary. I was a awful slow writer and thinker. And though I didn't put much in it, it tuk up plenty of time jes the same. I used to go around, too, a little with Corporal Murray Savage.

About this time we were going in again for bayonet practice. We had to rush the dummies the instructors set up and stab bayonets into them and muss them up. That sorter set me to worrying agin. I knowed the time was coming when I might have to do the same thing to the Germans. And though I knowed now that we were fighting for peace, still it made me feel queer to think I might have to cut up human beings. I still didn't want to kill. I still did feel somehow that it was wrong-terrible wrong for human beings to take each other's life. I don't know why I still felt like this. But I did jes the same.

June 26

Rambucourt, France.

We hiked a little ways and then taken the train for a short ride and then we got of train and hiked to Rambucourt and we stayed at Rambucourt until after dark and then we went up and took over the front line trenches for the first time.

CHAPTER 20

Americans Prepare

Editor's note:

The fundamental doctrine insisted upon by General Pershing is found in his statement of the general principles governing the training of units of the American Expeditionary Forces:

"The methods to be employed must remain or become distinctly our own.

"The general, principles governing combat remain unchanged in their essence. This war has developed special features which involve special phases of training, but the fundamental ideas enunciated in our Drill Regulations, Small Arms Firing Manual, Field Service Regulations and other service manuals remain the guide for both officers and soldiers and constitute the standard by which their efficiency is to be measured, except as modified in detail by instructions from these headquarters.

"The rifle and the bayonet are the principal weapons of the Infantry soldier. He will be trained to a high degree of skill as a marksman both on the target range and in field firing. An aggressive spirit must be developed until the soldier feels himself, as a bayonet fighter, invincible in battle."

Even while overseas, soldiers continued to drill.

The early period of training and trench warfare is thus described by Brigadier General Fox Conner, Chief G-3, General Headquarters:

"When the great German offensive of March, 1918, began, America had four divisions in the line. One of these (the 1st) held its own sector north of Toul while the 26th in the Chemin-des-Darnes, the 42nd in the Luneville, and the 2nd in the Verdun-St. Mihiel sectors were brigaded with the French for a first tour of duty in the trenches. Prior to the opening of the German offensive, the guiding principles which had been adopted for the employment of arriving divisions were in outline as follows:

"Arriving divisions would be sent to a training area (the artillery to one of the special camps) for a period of from one to two months. During this period the division was to be equipped, receive special training and become acclimated in the atmosphere of war. Upon the completion of this preliminary period the division was to be brigaded in quiet sectors with units of our Allies for a month or six weeks' duty in the trenches.

York had to live in trenches prior to entering combat zone.

"After this period of actual service the division was to be reassembled in a training area and receive a month's instruction in which attention would be especially devoted to maneuvering as a division. Upon the completion of this last month's instruction the division would take its place on the battle front. The German offensive, however, made necessary the abandonment of the policy above outlined. During the period to include July 15, 1918, it was essential to throw American troops into the fight at the earliest possible moment in order that the war might not be lost, and after July 15, it was only by the maximum use of American troops that winning the war in 1918 became possible. The 1st Division was therefore the only division which followed strictly the program originally intended.

"In September of 1917 it had been decided that the logical employment of the first American army to be formed was to be found in the reduction of the St. Mihiel salient. In preparation for this operation it had been arranged that as our divisions as such were ready to enter the line they should be placed on the St. Mihiel front, thus gradually creating a purely American sector. The German series of offensives and the necessity of breaking up those offensives at all costs-with corrollaries such as the desire, arising from necessity, of our Allies to raise the morale of their soldiers through the appearance of our soldiers at different parts of the front, and willingness of the British to increase our troop shipping provided our troops were sent to the British front for preliminary training-served, however, to upset our plans with regard to St. Mihiel for many weary months. In fact, by the end of June, 1918, our troops were literally spread from Switzerland to the English Channel and only the constant and firm determination of the Commander-in-Chief eventually to assemble our forces prevented that task from being abandoned as hopeless."

CHAPTER 21

Trench Warfare

At the commencement of the war no one intentionally thought the war would develop into a protracted stalemate of advancing from trench line to trench line. The trenches were hated by all soldiers on all sides. They became necessary evils to try to check the advance of armies into specific territories. The German VII Reserve Corps, pursued by the British Expeditionary Force during the battle of the Marne, dug the first trenches of the war. From the trenches, the Germans were able to halt the Allied advance. There followed what historians call the race to the sea; both armies marched north, trying to outflank each other, digging more trenches as they went. By the winter of 1914, the Western Front had become a narrow "ribbon of death," 475 miles long, stretching from the Belgian coast to Switzerland. The land between the two lines of trenches was called "No Man's Land."

A typical trench was about ten feet (three meters) deep. The French used wattle revetments (reinforcements) to stop the walls from caving in; the British and Germans used sandbags, corrugated iron, and wood.

Trenches were built in a zig-zag, forming a series of separate bays to limit the effect of shells bursting in the trenches and to stop the enemy from firing all the way along a trench if they captured part of it. Communication trenches stretched back to headquarters. Short cul-de-sacs, called saps poked out like fingers into "No Man's Land" to establish listening posts.

During 1915-1916, the generals on both sides tried to find a way to break through the lines of enemy trenches. But whereas each army had telephones, observation planes, machine guns, and railways to help them in their defense, their men still had to attack on foot, with rifles and bayonets. As the historian A. J. P Taylor pointed out, the armies had a 20th-century method of defense but a 19th-century method of attack. The result was that every advance against the heavily defended enemy trenches involved slaughter on a scale never before known.

Aerial view of zig-zag trenches.

In early 1915, the French lost 240,000 men while recapturing a handful of villages in Champagne. A British initiative at Neuve-Chapelle that spring was stopped by two German units with a dozen machine guns; the British troops, ordered to attack "regardless of loss," suffered 13,000 casualties.

Each soldier reacted in his own way to the pressures of trench warfare. Some found and enjoyed the excitement and comradeship they had anticipated: "I adore war; it's all the best fun one ever dreamed of," wrote Julien Grenfell.

But for others, the apparent futility of trench warfare began to change their image of war. Victors no longer seemed like heroes; victims—the men who went "over the top" to their deaths—earned admiration and sympathy. Many soldiers were bitter, angry, and depressed. "Heavy artillery fire continued through the night and the list of wounded grows ever bigger. Bad drinking water—I have got stomach pains and diarrhea. It is torture. Everybody is asking when we are going to be relieved," complained a German soldier. When the last member of British rifleman E. Chapman's platoon was killed (by a piece of shell that sliced off his head), Chapman found himself alone: "Giving up all hope of survival and feeling hopping mad, I waited with my Lewis gun for the enemy to come over the top." And it was always possible, as the French novelist Henri Barbusse described in 1917, to come upon a wounded soldier standing upright, rooted to the spot, terrified, "a sort of screaming tree."

Many soldiers found that "it is worse than useless to think about things" and simply tried, as one French soldier wrote, "to carry oneself correctly." Others "switched off" from the horror around them and wrote home using the cheerful triteness they might have read in the newspapers.

The following is a remarkable experience of an American told by Romeo Houle of the First Canadian Division.

This story reveals in all its realism the reason why America entered the Great War—to save the world from the suffering herein described. Every American who reads this true account will understand, as never before, the feeling that Americans began to have towards the German leaders for perpetrating the German War. They were viewed as despots who forced this horror upon civilization. To bring this war to an end, the Americans crossed the seas to fight with the Allies and save humanity. This true story of the trenches is undeniably one of the most poignant human documents that the great struggle has produced.

Romeo Houle was born in New Bedford, Mass., Oct. 29th, 1893, the son of a local barber, Zacharie Houle, and Xeline Bagnoche. He has a common school education. He moved to Montreal in 1912, where he was a barber. When war was declared he enlisted in the Sixty-fifth Regiment, First Canadian Division, Aug. 10, 1914. His father secured the young soldier's discharge through Congressman Walsh of Massachusetts on the ground that he was an American citizen and was not of age when he enlisted. He made notes of his experiences while in the trenches, and the subjoined production was written by him for Current History in collaboration with his friend Arthur L. Bouvier, editor of a French newspaper at New Haven.

"The true story of the trenches has never been told. I know, because for many months I have lived in trenches. I have slept daily in dread of bullet, shrapnel, mine, and deadly gas; and nightly in fear of mine and gas and the man-eating rats.

I am one of the few soldiers living who entered the front trenches at the opening of the war and who lived to fight the Germans in the front trenches in February, 1916. Of my original company (the Fourth of the Fourteenth Battalion, Third Brigade, First Canadian Division), which marched away to that hell at Laventie and Ypres so gaily—500 brave boys—I am one of the sixteen who survive.—

Who has seen hell? Who has experienced the horrors of Milton's terrible vision or the slow tortures of Dante's inferno? God! If Dante's dream madness were truth, and those seven circles were seven encircling battle lines in Northern France or the torn fringe of brave little Belgium, I could stand up and say there is no agony of body or mind which I have not seen, which I have not experienced. I thank God and give Him the glory that I still am sane. Gas? What do you knew of it, you people who never heard earth and heaven rock with the frantic turmoil of the ceaseless bombardment? A crawling yellow cloud that pours in upon you, that gets you by the throat and shakes you as a huge mastiff might shake a kitten, and leaves you burning in every nerve and vein of your body with pain unthinkable; your eyes starting from their sockets; your face turned yellow-green.

Rats? What did you ever read of the rats in the trenches? Next to gas, they still slide on their fat bellies through my dreams. Poe could have got new inspiration from their dirty hordes. Rats, rats, rats—I see them still, slinking from new meals on corpses, from Belgium to the Swiss Alps. Rats, rats, rats, tens of thousands of rats, crunching between battle lines while the rapid-firing guns mow the trench edge—crunching their hellish feasts. Full fed, slipping and sliding down into the wet trenches they swarm at night—and more than one poor wretch has had his face eaten off by them while he slept.

Stench? Did you ever breathe air foul with the gases arising from a thousand rotting corpses? Dirt? Have you ever fought half madly through days and nights and weeks unwashed, with feverish rests between long hours of agony, while the guns boom their awful symphony of death, and the bullets zip-zip-zip ceaselessly along the trench edge that is your skyline—and your deathline, too, if you stretch and stand upright?

You wouldn't believe all I have seen, all I have left. Ah, no; you would say, "Romeo Houle, you are lying," were I to tell you some unbelievable things that I have really lived through. Men go mad over there. When you know what life in the first-line trenches is like you will wonder that I have returned, and that, having returned, I am still in my right mind. Sometimes, at night, I find myself again carrying the wounded back after the charge, and listening to dying soldiers telling me to look into blood-soaked pockets for last letters to their sweethearts or mothers back home. "Tell mother that I received the Blessed Sacrament before the battle began." I hear their breaking voices whisper, "Tell mother," while the thundering artillery pours its curtain of fire upon us, and our boys throw back from their rude, hand-made sling shots their deadly "jam-pots." "Tell mother!" I think all the battle front is crying now those words. Oh, Mother of God, hear them and end this needless butchery!

I fought at Ypres. I fought at St. Julien. I fought at Lacouture and Festubert. I fought at Cuinchy. I fought at Givenchy and La Bassee, and in the first-line trenches at Messines. And before all these I fought in the first line at Richebourg and Laventie, and I live, 1 of 16 alive out of 500."

CHAPTER 22

We is Goin' in to Fight

Clogged roads made it difficult to get into position.

June 26 Rambucourt, France

We were going in at last. We could hear the guns away in the distance now, jes like the thunder in the hills at home. We seed a right-smart lot of deserted trenches with wire entanglements, all snarled and mussed up. We seed gun emplacements half full of water. We passed an awful lot of graves, with little wooden crosses at their heads. I'm a-tellin' you that brought it home to us. And all the roads were sorter blocked up with troops coming and going and artillery and transports. As we got up closer we could hear the rifles barking and the machine guns spitting, and soon the bullets started coming over. They were stray bullets. The Germans were firing in the front line ahead of us and they were missing the parapet and coming right back among us. It was the first time that we were under fire, and of course we were a little nervous. The officers told us boys that it was all right; that they were only stray bullets; that they would not injure us, and not to mind them. And one of them-there Italian boys grinned and give as his opinion that it didn't matter whether they were strays or not, that if they hit us they would do jes as much damage as if they was aimed at us. As we got right up close some of the boys began to duck as the bullets come over. And then somebody else 'lowed that it weren't no use ducking nohow, because you never hear the one that hits you. We went in and takened over the front line at night time.

June 27

Montsec Sector, France.

We releaved the 26th Div. Boys at night in the Montsec Sector at Rambucourt and we stayed there until the 4th of July. The Greeks and Italians and all of the other boys done fairly well. They shore were turning out to be the bestest soldiers. I was often out on "No Man's Land". I done done some patrolling. I handled an automatic squad. We were armed with French sho-sho rifles. They were sort of portable machine guns. They fired about eighteen shots without reloading. They were not much good nohow. They were big and clumsy. They were too heavy. They were not accurate or silent. You never could be shore you would hit what you fired at, no matter how good a shot you were. All you could do with them was make a lot of noise, and waste a heap of ammunition, and hope for the best. They weren't near as good as the sawed-off shotguns.

French machine guns were unreliable.

We had a heap of big stuff from the artillery coming over and some gas, and we had to put on them pesky gas masks agin. The German snipers were always after us. They were good marksmen. They could bust a periscope ‘most every shot. They knowed how to keep our heads down, too. The bullets was always coming over, humming and buzzing around our ears, jes like a lot of mad hornets or bumble bees when you rob their nests.

I did a heap of thinking and praying at this time. And more’n ever I jes knowed I was going to get back all right. I believed in God and in His promises. And I knowed as as I did that He would believe in and watch over me, and there one night in that old front line trench, I wrote in my diary:

July 1
Montsec Sector, France.

I few words on Christian witness in war and why a Christian does worry. Yet there is no use worrying about anything except, the worry of So many Souls who have passed out into the Deep of an Unknown world and has left no testimony as to the welfair of their souls. There is no use of worrying a Bout Shells for you cant keep them from bursting in your trench nor you cant Stop the rain or prevent a light from a going up jes as you are half way over the parapet-So what is the use of worrying if you cant alter things just ask God to help you and accept them and make the best of them by the help of God; yet some men do worry and by doing so they effectually destroy their peace of Mind without doing any one any good. Yet it is often the religious man who worries. I have even heard those whose care was for the Soldier Soul Deplore the fact that he Did not worry. I have heard it said that the Soldier is so Careless, realizes his, position So little.

Front line religion was very important to many soldiers.

Up there in the front line I knowed as I had never knowed before what a comforting thing religion is. So I clung to my faith all the time. I read my Testament everywhere. I read it in the dugouts, in the fox holes, in the front lines and everywhere. Hit was my rock to cling to; hit and my diary.

The trouble with our boys when we went into this quiet sector was they would want to go out on top of the trenches and start something. They was wanting to get into it and get it over. I knowed now that the Greeks and Italians and Poles and New York Jews were fighters. Ho! Ho! As right-smart fighters as the American-borned boys. They didn't want to lay around and do nothing. And they would even go on top and get the Germans out. Once one of them come up to me right there in the front line and asked me, "Where is the war?"

They was always wanting to go over the top-and keep a-going. They shore were ambitious.

Well, we would stay in a quiet sector for a few days. Then we would pull out and hike off to another, and then another, until we gradually worked our way into the real fighting sectors.

July 4

Cormeville, France.

Then we come out to Cormeville and stayed there until July 17th.

July 17

Rambucourt, France.

Went Back in the Lines again and stayed until July 25th.

August 8

Mandres, France.

While we were in these so-called quiet sectors four of our men were detailed to take the chow to the front line outposts. It was night time, of course. They were given the necessary pass-words. But one of them, on the return, got separated and also forgot the passwords. This was serious. Then he done something which sorter showed the kind of soldier he was. He waited quietly for about a half hour until another soldier come along. He then halted him in the customary way, advanced him, received the password, and let him pass by. He done pretended he was on guard duty and so done received the password and got back all right. He was a Greek and he spoke very little English, but that didn't stop him nohow. I'm a-telling you that's soldiering for you; that's using your head!

The Greeks and Italians and Poles and New York Jews. Ho! Ho!—they were men. I was beginning to understand them.

Editor's note: (The 82nd Division was called the Rainbow Division, since it was made up of various nationalities.)

Pont-á-Mousson, France, as York saw it August 16, 1918.

Went to Pont-á-Mousson and stayed there, in the front until August 24th.

To we-uns all dirty and tired from being in the front-line trenches and hiking all over France, Pont-á-Mousson was a kinder earthly paradise. It is in the valley on the banks of the Moselle River. It was late summer, jes the time when the fruit is ready for picking. The trees and vines were loaded with grapes and apples and everything. The gardens were all kept up nice, with everything kinder ripe and ready, and there was plenty of green grass and shade and cool, clean water. It was most hard for us to imagine that we were still in the war. The city wasn't mussed up at all. It hadn't been shelled nohow. We heard there had been a kind of agreement between the French and the Germans to leave it alone. So it had stayed there all by itself and unharmed for four years. We bathed and rested there. And got us some good fruit and laid out in the sunshine until we felt sort of re-made all over again.

September 1
Pont-á-Mousson, France.

When we entered the town this time we found that the French population had jes left before we arrived. Everything was left standing jes as it was. Even the tables were set and the food was still standing on the stoves. Some of us stole in and had the best food we done tasted for a long time. The beds were made; everything was clean and orderly. You see the French population had been done told that the drive was beginning, and they had lit out as fast as they could, only taking with them what they could tote in their arms. About this time the Germans started to send over some big shells. They done done a whole heap of damage to the nice little town and they done mussed up the orchards and done scattered the fruit all over the place. A little while later we heard the most awful explosion, jes as if an ammunition dump had been blowed up. We found out that our artillery done moved up some big naval guns. They were much bigger than tractors, and most awful long. They shore let the Germans have it. We could hear the big shells whinin' and whizzin' over our heads on their way to Metz, which was fifteen miles away.

We were now getting ready for the St. Mihiel drive, which was to be the first real battle we were in, and the first major offensive for the American Army. It done opened with a most awful barrage from our big guns. It was the awfulest thing you ever heard. It made the air tremble and the ground shake. At times you couldn't hear your own voice nohow. The air was full of airplanes, and most of them American planes. There must have been hundreds of them. They were diving and circling around all over the place like a swarm of birds. We seed several right-smart fights away up there above us. One day we was sitting in a trench, looking up and watching, when one of them-there East Side Jews 'lowed that he might be killed in a airplane accident, but if ever he was, the airplane would have to light on him. For a few days before the attack we waited on a little hillside jes outside of Pont-á-Mousson, on the banks of the river. Then we moved up into the front-line trenches. We waited in them about a day and a night until the artillery done done its work, and it done done it right smart, too.

CHAPTER 23

The Battle of St. Mihiel

View of St. Mihiel as
York saw it September 12, 1918.

Editor's notes:

Examination of a map of the western theater of war during any period after the initial rush of the Gremans into France will show at the eastern end of the battle line a sharp triangle reaching into French territory with its eastern end at a little town called Pont-á-Mousson, on the German border just south of Metz, its apex at St. Mihiel; and the other leg of the triangle reaching off to the northwest behind Verdun. This salient had been created at the time of the initial invasion of France. It had persisted throughout the long and savage battles for Verdun. The French had repeatedly sought to iron it out, but without avail. Now, as the railroads from the American bases on the channel ran directly toward that spot, and as the largest American prisoner of war camps was at Toul just south of the salient, it therefore motivated the American army to secure the area and set the American soldiers free.

In his official report, General Pershing said that the reduction of the St. Mihiel salient had been planned as the first independent American offensive action on a large scale. The disposition of troops in preparation for it began as early as August 30th, and before its completion entailed preparations which the General Pershing describes thus:

"The preparation for a complicated operation again the formidable defenses in front of us included the assembling of divisions and of corps and army artillery transport, aircraft, tanks, ambulances, the location of hospitals, and the molding together of all of the elements of a great modern army with its own railheads, supplied directly by our own Service of Supplies The concentration for this operation, which was to be a surprise, involved the movement, mostly night, of approximately 600,000, troops, and required for its success the most careful attention to every detail."

The first major action by an all-American army was that which began before the St. Mihiel salient September 11, 1918. The Germans had occupied that salient almost four years, and had built it into what they believed to be an impregnable position. The Americans, under direct command of General Pershing, reduced it in a three days' advance.

The salient was a huge bulge, almost twenty miles in depth, turning southwest from Combres at the north base and Hattonville at the south and looping down around the towns of St. Mihiel and Ailly. It was powerfully held by masses of enemy troops.

General Pershing's army attacked from the west, south and east all the way from Bonzee to Norroy, and by September 13th had pushed it back to a straight line drawn from Combres to Hattonville. The French attacked at Ailly, the apex of the salient as it was on September 11.

The entire operation was conducted with rapidity and with

irresistible energy. The dash and enthusiasm of the American soldiers astonished and delighted the French and British as completely as it staggered the Germans.

By September 13th the Americans had taken forty-seven towns and villages, reduced the German front from forty miles to twenty, captured the railway that connects Verdun with Commercy, opened the cities of Nancy and Toul to the allies, and with the French and British on the east, created a new battle front on a line running from Hattonville on the west to Pagny on the east Pagny—being a town on the Moselle river, at the German border.

The importance of this victory could hardly be overestimated. It opened the way, and was followed up by the demolition of the whole German line from the Swiss border to the North Sea, and hastened the great German retreat. In the action itself, September 11 to 13, about 15,000 Germans were taken prisoner by the Americans.

York continues his experience as follows:

September 12
St. Mihiel, France

The Big American Drive started and we went over the top the night of the 12th then we took a little town By the name of Norroy and went on to the top of another hill Beyond Norroy.

Early on the morning of the twelfth the guns let down a most awful heavy barrage, louder than a thunderstorm. And at daybreak we went over the top. We cut our way through the barbed wire and advanced on the little village of Norroy. But fast as we went forward the Germans kept on moving backwards, faster. They jes wouldn't stand and fight it out. Our battalion was right in the thick of it, and some of the other companies got mussed up right smart, but ours never lost a man. I don't know why, but we didn't. I'm a-thinking the Germans were in too much of a hurry to take careful aim. There was a-plenty of machine-gun and artillery fire, but it didn't seem to find us. I done heard tell that it takes nearly a ton of lead to kill a man in a war. I kinder believe it. There were bullets and shells everywhere, but the boys kept on a-going. None of them fell. There was no holding that-there League of Nations of ours. They wanted to push right on and not stop until they got to Berlin. They cussed the Germans out for not standing and they kept yelling at them to wait and fight it out. We continued from Norroy on to the top of the hill beyond until we got in advance of our own flank and the Germans were enfilading us. So we was ordered by our Captain to dig in until some of the other troops got up.

When we captured Norroy we mopped up the houses and went through the town looking for prisoners. A lot of our boys takened prisoner several barrels of wine. So they knocked the bungs out of them and drinked a whole mess of it. Then they were fuller of fight than ever. And there was one big house there, all locked up. It looked like headquarters, but when we done surrounded it and stormed it we found it was a storehouse and it was full of Belgian hares. These hares ran all over the place and our boys done chased them. I'm a-telling you those barrels of wine and them-there, hares shore demoralized my Greeks and Italians. And when we started back in the night one of the boys takened a milk goat that was captured and was leading it back to Pont-á-Mousson. And when the officer done called to him and asked him what he was doing with that goat, he answered: "Sir, I am jes going back to put a little cream in my coffee."

When we dug in the hillside beyond Norroy we seen a little vineyard. We were very hungry, and them-there grapes jes natcherly made our mouths water. So we begun to slip back after the grapes, but the Germans had an observation balloon, one of those big sausage balloons, up in the air, and they seed us and directed the German artillery to tech us off. So we had orders not to go back there any more. But that night I decided to go back and get me some of them grapes. I jes stalked back and was keeping very quiet so I wouldn't be seen when a shell landed near and I jumped and ran and I done run right into my own Captain, Captain Danforth of Augusta, Ga. He liked grapes, too—Ho! Ho!—and we both fled.

The Germans threw a lot of gas shells into Norroy, and we had to wear our gas masks for several hours. I had been made corporal before this battle. So I led the squad. I kinder think they almost led me. I mean I was supposed to be in the front and they were supposed to follow. But no matter how fast I went they wanted to go faster, so that they could get at the Germans. The Greeks and Italians, the Poles and the Jews and the other city boys were still firing pretty wild. They were still mostly hitting the ground or the sky. They burned up a most awful lot of Uncle Sam's ammunition. But they kept on a-going jes the same. They were that full of fight that wild cats shore would have backed away from them.

The St. Mihiel offensive must have been as complete a drive and as well arranged as ever could have been by any general of any army. It was a great success. The feeling of the majority of the boys was one hundred per cent. for General Pershing. As a whole the Army was back of him, believed in him, and would follow him anywhere. They seemed to think as a general he was a right-smart success. After a few days in the front lines we were takened out to rest in a little valley jes back of Pont-á-Mousson. But I never did hear of that-there goat any more. I don't know whether the boy got the cream for his coffee or not.

On September 24, York traveled this path towards the battle trenches of St. Mihiel. St. Mihiel commanded a view that the Germans did not want to surrender without a fight to try to retain it.

Editor's note:

The American Army was disposed to move into battle like a pair of pincers, and the enemy was indeed pinched. One tip pincers was near Pont-á-Mousson, the other just south of Verdun on the Meuse. The pivot between the two was at St. Mihiel and each arm of the pincers was about ten miles long. After the artillery had made play for some four hours these two arms began coming together, not at all slowly but irresistibly. From one claw-tip to the other was about thirty miles.

It took two days to bring the two together, but it was accomplished and thereby about two hundred square miles of French territory was captured from the Germans. When the closing movement began this bit of land had held about 100,000 of the enemy but he slipped away with all the speed he might. The hardest fighting took place on the southern leg of the salient, running northward toward Thiaucourt. The terrain there was low and marshy and the field before the advancing Americans was swept by fire from the French forts. The very hardest fighting occurred on the west side of the salient on a hillside called Les Esparges. This had been assaulted by the French repeatedly in the past but to no avail. Now after vigorous artillery preparation French and Americans together swept up the slope in a rush that never stopped until they had reached the top of a series of elevations that extended almost to St. Mihiel and that because of its commanding height had been of the utmost strategic advantage to the Germans. Barbed wire, dense brush, and innumerable nest had to be met and overcome, but the assailants were equal to all. The American artillery practice was credited with playing a great part in the victory. The hall of shells cut the barbed wire and mowed down the trees and bushes that impeded the path. It is not altogether gratifying to our national pride, however, to learn from General Pershing's report that while the gunners were ours the guns belonged to the French—we were not yet able to equip our troops with this most essential arm.

It may be doubted whether any victory of equal proportions during the great war was so speedily won. Within two days the Germans were driven out of the salient, while those who were slow to go had been captured. At one point a whole Hun regiment was surrendered in a body with all its officers, and to expedite matters, after the men had been relieved of their arms, the regiment was marched to the rear under command of its own chiefs, and with a few American cavalrymen riding alongside like stockmen riding herd. Everywhere were stacks of abandoned munitions and supplies. At one point a big American shell had exploded on a railway just in time to stop the progress of a retiring train with twenty-two cars loaded with machine guns, big guns, and ammunition. Unhappily no such fortunate shot stopped the thievish enemy carrying away loot. It is said that at few laces along the battle-line did the Germans give fuller play to their destructive and thievish proclivities than at Thiaucourt which they had occupied for four years. The banks had been plundered first by "requisitions" and at the last moment by the simpler process of breaking open the vaults and taking all that was there. Metal of every sort, church bells, statues, water pipes, kitchen utensils were seized and sent back to Germany. And when they were finally whipped, and every responsible officer must have known that the war was ended, they fled, destroying practically everything that they could not carry away. This was one of the reasons why American soldiers listened with cynical indifference to the cry for aid which the Germans set up twenty-four hours after the armistice was signed.

September 17
St. Mihiel, France.

We come out to some wood and camped there and got us something to eat.

September 23
St. Mihiel, France.

We come on back to some more woods and then we stayed a few days.

September 24
St. Mihiel, France.

We started for the Argonne forest. We takened a little narrow gauge railroad to a place somewhere in France. We didn't know where it was. I don't think anybody except the officers

knowed that. Here we come upon about one hundred old French buses. They were big and painted white. The drivers were Chinese and most of them spoke French. I done never seen Chinaman before, and I jes couldn't keep my eyes off them. Some of our boys afterwards done told the story, I don't know how true it was, that one of them-there Chinamen kept a-pesterin' one of our doughboys for a souvenir. The doughboy took a Mills grenade out of his pocket—one of them pesky little things. You pull the lever and in five seconds it explodes. Well, he pulled the lever and then handed it to the Chinaman and told him to put it to his ear and listen to it tick. Ho! Ho!

Them Chinamen were the awfulest drivers you ever seed. They must have sorter had the idea they had to get us there before they even started. The way they done tore and bumped those old French buses over those old French roads was enough to make your hair stand up straight. I'm a-thinking we were in more danger from them than we were from the Germans when we were in the front line. Two of the trucks turned over, but nobody was mussed up bad. It now seemed to me that we had most all of the nationalities in the world around, and there were all them-there different races in my platoon. There were the American-borned and the foreign-borned boys; there were the French and those Chinese drivers and the Germans over the way. Hit shore was a lot of travelling and meeting people for a mountain boy who never travelled more'n a few miles before he left home.

Although York did not have much in common with his men, he grew to love them and care for them.

The war brings out the worst in you. It turns you into a mad, fightin' animal, but it also brings out something else, something I jes don't know how to describe, a sort of tenderness and love for the fellows fightin' with you. It's sort of clean, like a fire of pine logs on a frosty night. I had kinder got to know and sorter understand the boys around me. I knowed their weakness as well as their strength. I guess they knowed mine. If you live together for several months sharing and sharing alike, you learn a heap about each other. It was as though we could look right through each other and knowed everything without anything being hid. I'm a-telling you I loved them-there boys in my squad. I had forgiven them for their bad shooting. I had forgiven it if they drank and tore things up before going to the front. Anyway, that was their own business. It was no affair of mine. If they got happiness that way, it was all right with me. I guess they sorter figured they were going to be mussed up and maybe killed when they got into the trenches, so they figured they might jes as well enjoy things while they had the chance. If that's the way they figured it out, it was all right with me. If they cussed a whole lot, I don't think they meant it to be as bad as it sounded. It was their own way of expressing themselves; that's all. Even if a fellow doesn't drink or smoke or cuss, like me for instance, he has no right to find fault with others, provided they don't interfere with him. He has no right to pass judgment, and I didn't nohow. I kinder think away down underneath I sorter loved them for their weakness most of all. They were my buddies. That's a word that's only understood by soldiers who have lived under the same blankets, gathered around the same chow can, and looked at death together. I never knowed I loved my brother-man so much until I was a doughboy. I knowed men could be strong and rough, but I never understood before that they could be so tender and loving, and I jes couldn't baar to think of anything happenin' to them. It was too awful to think of them-there boys being wounded or killed. I kinder did a lot of thinking and praying about these things as we moved out into the Argonne. Somehow, I seemed to jes know that we were going to get into it right, in them-there Woods.

October 3
Zona Woods, France.

We camped over night on a high hill in the woods.

October 4
Argonne Forest, France.

Machine gun nest in the Argonne Woods.

We had went on into the Argonne Woods where we stayed over night. The battle of the Argonne started the night of the 25th of September, but we were sorter in reserve. We camped each night well back in the woods and moved up a little bit at a time. At first we noticed the woods hadn't been shot up much. We hadn't reached the main battlegrounds. But as we got closer, I'm a-telling you we knowed there was a war on. The woods were all mussed up and the ground was all torn up with shells.

We went out on the main road and lined up and started for the front and the germans was shelling the road and airoplanes was humming over our heads and we were stumbling over dead horses and dead men and shells were Bursting all around me and then it was that I could see the Power of God helped man if he would only trust him. Oh it was there I could look up and say:

> *"0 Jesus, the great rock of foundation Where on my feet were set with sovereign grace; Through Shells or Death with all their agitation Thou wilt protect me if I will only trust in thy Grace Bless thy holy name."*

132 Prisners So you can
See here in this case
of mine where god helped
me out I had Bin
living for god and
working in church
work some time Before
I come to the army
So I am a witness
to the fact that god
Did help me out of
that hard Battle for
the Bushes were shot
off all around me
and I never got a
scratch So you can
See that god will Be
with you if you will
only Trust him and

(33.)

THE FAITH THAT MOVETH MOUNTAINS

In this extraordinary entry in his war diary, scribbled the night after the fight, Sergeant York says that God helped him in his fight with the German machine guns.

CHAPTER 24

The Argonne Fight

"We layed in some little holes on the roadside all day while bombs were bursting all around us."

October 7
Argonne Forest, France.

We layed in some little holes on the roadside all Day that night we went and stayed a little while and come Back to our little holes and the Shells Bursting all around us. I seen men just blowed up By the Big German Shells Which Were Bursting all around us. So the order came for us to take hill223 and 240 the 8th.

It was raining a little bit all day, kinder drizzly and very damp. Lots of big shells bursting all around us. We were not up close enough for the machine guns to reach us, but airplanes were buzzing overhead 'most all the time, jes like a lot of hornets. Lots of men were killed by the artillery fire. And lots were wounded. We seed quite a lot of our machine-gun battalion across the road from us blowed up by the big shells. The woods were all mussed up and looked as if a terrible cyclone done swept through them. But God would never be cruel enough to create a cyclone as terrible as that Argonne battle. Only man would ever think of doing an awful thing like that. It looked like the "Abomination of Desolation" must have been. And all through the long night those big guns flashed and growled jes like the lightning and the thunder when it storms in the mountains at home. And oh, my! we had to pass the wounded. And some of them were on stretchers going back to the dressing stations and some of them were lying around moaning and twitching. And oh, my! the dead were all along the road and their mouths were open and their eyes, too, but they couldn't see nothing no more nohow. And it was wet and cold and damp. And it all made me think of the Bible and the story of the anti-Christ and Armageddon. And I'm a-telling you the little log cabin in Wolf Valley in old Tennessee seemed a long, long way off.

The partially damaged Argonne Forest as York saw it. These sights reminded him of many Bible passages describing the destruction of the last days.

Editor's note:

The Forest of the Argonne, in which the fiercest fighting of this period occurred, was itself admirably fitted for defensive purposes. It was dense with underbrush cut up by gullies and out cropping of limestone ridges, with but few dark and almost impenetrable roads. No ordinary defensive work was this, but a network of trenches, big and little, guarded in front by wire enough to fence in a whole nation. Furthermore, they were concreted, and provided with bombproof dugouts, some of which attained a degree of comfort amounting to luxury, thanks to the neighboring homes which the Germans had despoiled of the furniture and even pictures. Some had electric lighted tunnels reaching far back into the streets of a neighboring town whereby the defenders might go out to seek rest and arousement in safety. Much of the line was constructed of solid masonry, reenforced with bars of steel. The defenders had foreseen that their assailants would rely largely upon tanks in the attack and had made preparations for them. Walls were built across all roads of masonry sufficiently heavy to withstand even the forceful push of a tank. Traps dug deep in the earth were cunningly concealed by a surface layer that would give way immediately upon feeling the weight of a tank. Barbed wire was everywhere and back of this wire were machine guns innumerable that started up with their murderous crackle the instant the wire was touched. And back of it all were not less than 350,000 of the best German troops whose numbers were steadily increased as the battle progressed.

The accounts of some eye-witnesses of this struggle may be fitly quoted to round out General Pershing's official account as reported by Edwin L. James from the New York Times.

"Turn your attention to the all-night fighting in the Argonne Forest, and realize what our men are going through. It is raining and there is inky darkness. The boche is shelling heavily and pouring gas into all the valleys. Our men must

travel on the hills. Those hills are being raked by thousands of German 77s.

The Americans in the advance hit the barbed wire. Rifles are slung across shoulders and pliers are pulled out. Busily our men cut wire after wire. The noise they make brings the nasty rat-a-tat of a Hun machine gun from a tree on the other side of the wire. Then another and another, and twenty machine guns are going.

Their aim is poor, and their flashes give our rifles a chance. Our doughboys pile through that wire fence and through the underbrush and stack up against another fence ten feet farther on. The range has been telephoned back to the boche batteries and shells begin to fall all around.

They cut that barbed wire and then stumble on to concealed wire entanglements covered with brush. They climb these. All the time, from the dark, German snipers and machine gun men, always with time enough to fall back, are taking their toll. Now our line comes upon a broad trench with more wire. In the dark our boys leap across it; some fall into it. Others get over at the first attempt and pull out their pliers to cut more wires.

All this time it is raining and cold, very cold. The inky blackness there in the forest is broken by streams of fire from machine guns and the intermittent flash of some German sniper, seeming to taunt the youthful Americans struggling against such devilish odds.

It takes stout hearts, it takes real men to stand this. But it was over two and a half miles of this sort of terrain that one American division tore its way through the Argonne Forest. This was the worst part. Farther on the wire was less frequent, and our men in the Argonne, having crashed through the Bois d'Apremont, are now reaching a zone where the roads are good, and the advance is easier. Since the French tried vainly to take it in 1915 the Germans had used the Argonne Forest as a rest area—a sort of recreation ground for their war-worn troops, and had built such defenses as they thought would defy all attempts frontally. For three years the Argonne has been a kind of pleasure resort for boche fighters. It is worth years of any ones life to see what they had built there on the pretty wooded slopes and through tangles of verdant beauty.

There were underground palaces with electric illumination and with hotel ranges to cook for the officers. On a slope just a mile back of the front line there is an enormous cave fronting north. Its front was built of brownstone, on which had been chased pillars and other carvings. Above its big portals was the word "Offizierhaus," and above that an enormous iron cross. In this club there were a large dining hall and perhaps ten rooms. The inside was lined with concrete and wooden floors had been laid. At the dining table were mahogany chairs, [stolen] from some nearby French chateau. Over the General's place hung an electric call bell, and electric lights were strung down the middle of the table. It represented the luxury of war. This was just one of hundreds and hundreds of these dug-in and scientifically made dwelling places."

The progress of the Argonne-Meuse offensive is divided by General Pershing in his report into three parts, and between his accounts of these he diverges to tell the story of the work of the Americans on the more western battle fronts. We may, however, proceed with the Argonne story to its completion. October 4th began what the General calls the second phase of the Argonne fight. Differing little in character from the earlier fighting, it continued until October 10th when the wood was wholly cleared of the enemy.

Ammunition train, 82nd Div., near Chatel Chehery, October, 1918. York was supplied from these ammunition stations which followed the soldiers at a distance.

Alvin York writes:

October 8, 1917
Argonne Forest, France.

So the morning of the 8th just before daylight we started for the hill at Chatel Chehery. So before we got there it got light and the germans sent over a heavy Barrage and also gas and we put on our gas mask and just Pressed right on through those shells and got to the top of hill 223 to where we was to start over the top at 6:10 A.M.

All day long on October 7th we laid out there in the rain and the mud along the main army road running from Varennes to Fleville, and watching the attack of the First Battalion, which takened Hill 223 in the afternoon. Shells were bursting all around and a whole heap of stray bullets were buzzing through the air. Airplanes were fighting overhead. It was all most awful.

Fearful dogfights overhead were unnerving to York who had not even seen an airplane before the war.

Through most of the night we laid out there, too. It was that dark you couldn't see nothing nohow. Lights were flashing from the gun fire. There were all sorts of sounds and noises. It was raining worse'n than ever. The ground was soft and mucky and all cut up. We were wet through and dirty and kinder tired. About 3 A.M. in the morning, the morning of October 8th, our Captain, Captain Danforth, come to us and told us we were to move on to Hill 223, which was to be the jumping-off place for our attack, which was to be at daybreak. Our objective was the Decauville Railroad, which was about three kilometres to the northwest of the hill, and further on almost in the centre of the Argonne Forest. We were to bust that old railroad so as to stop the Germans from sending in their troops and supplies. With the Captain leading, we marched over the Aire River on a little shaky, wooden bridge which the engineers had thrown up for us, on through the town of Chatel Chehery and on up to Hill 223. It was so dark and everything was so mussed up and the going was so rough that it was most awful hard to keep contact and to find the hill. But we done kept on a-going jes the same. We were marching, I might say floundering around, in column of squads.

"With the Captain leading, we marched over the Aire River on a little shaky, wooden bridge which the engineers had thrown up for us, on through the town of Chatel Chehery and on up to Hill 223."

The noise were worse than ever, and everybody was shouting through the dark, and nobody seemed to be able to hear what anybody else said. We should have reached the hill before daybreak. But we didn't. It weren't nobody's fault. The going was too tough. So as soon as they were able to see the German artillery lit into us with a heap of big stuff. One of their shells bust plumb in the middle of one of our squads, and wounded or killed every man. They done laid down the meanest kind of a barrage too, and the air was jes full of gas. But we put on our masks and kept plugging and slipping and sliding, or falling into holes and tripping over all sorts of things and getting up again and stumbling on for a few yards and then going down again, until we done reached the hill. The First Battalion had takened it the day before, but they hadn't mopped it up. And there were some snipers and German machine guns left there hidden in the brush and in fox holes.

Machine gun sniper

And they sniped at us a whole heap. I guess we must have run over the top of some of them, too, because a little later on we were getting fire from the rear. We were to go over the top at 6:10 A.M. and push on across the valley and work our way across the ridges to that-there old railroad. The Captain's orders was for two of our platoons to go over the top first and advance as a front wave with the other two platoons in support following about one hundred yards behind the front wave. I was in the left supporting platoon. Hit was the extreme left of our division and was supposed to keep contact with the Twenty-eighth Division, which was on our left, but we never did see anything of them all that morning. I guess they must have run into some awful tough fighting and been held up for a while.

"Going over the top" into the heat of enemy fire.

Well, at the zero hour, which was 6:10 A.M., with fixed bayonets, we done, went over the, top, as ordered. Our boys was to give us a Barrage. So the time came and no Barrage and we had to go with out one. So we started over the top at 6:10 A.M. and the germans was Putting their machine guns to working all over the hill in front of us and on our left and right. So I was in suport and I could see my pals getting picked off until it almost looked like there was none left.

I don't know what happened to our artillery support, but we didn't get none nohow, except from a lieutenant from the Third Battalion. He done stood near six-foot-six tall. And he come up on top of the hill, dragging what looked like a toy cannon with him. It was a trench mortar. He did the best he could with it, but it didn't help much nohow. The Germans met our charge across the valley with a regular sleet storm of bullets. I'm a-telling you that-there valley was a death trap. It was a triangular-shaped valley with steep ridges covered with brush, and swarming with machine guns on all sides. I guess our two waves got about halfway across and then jes couldn't get no further nohow. The Germans done got us and they done got us right smart. They jes stopped us in our tracks. Their machine guns were up there on the heights overlooking us and well hidden, and we couldn't tell for certain where the terrible heavy fire was coming from. It 'most seemed as though it was coming from everywhere. I'm a-telling you they were shooting straight, and our boys jes done went down like the long grass before the mowing machine at home. Our attacks jes faded out.

We had to lie down flat on our faces and dig in. And there we were out there in the valley all mussed up and unable to get any further with no barrage to help us, and that-there German machine-gun fire and all sorts of big shells and gas cutting us to pieces. There was scarcely none of our front wave left. Lieutenant Stewart, who was leading the platoon in front of where I was lying, went down with a shot through the leg, but got up again and rallied the few men he had left and led them forward until he fell dead with a bullet through the head. I couldn't see Captain Danforth. He was on the other side of the hill on the right. I could hear shells and machine guns there, too, and I knowed he was getting it jes as bad as we was.

York and his patrol were pinned down.

The German machine guns had done stopped our attack. We jes couldn't go on. We could scarcely even lift up our heads as we laid flat on the ground. But all the time we knowed we had to get through to that railroad somehow. We jes had to.

About this time we figured that the worstest machine-gun fire was coming from a ridge over on our left front. We knowed then that them-there machine guns would have to be put out of action before the advance could go on. We also knowed that there was so many of them and they were in such commanding positions that a whole battalion couldn't put them out of action nohow by a frontal attack. I doubt if a whole division could get to them that way. But they had to be takened somehow.

Our platoon sergeant, Harry M. Parsons, from Brooklyn, N. Y., done exposed himself again and again, trying to locate exactly where the machine guns over there on the left front were firing from. He hadn't no chance nohow of getting in touch with the Captain. He had to use his own judgment. He done done it. He ordered the left half of our platoon to crawl back a little and try and work out way down around on the left and then push on through the heavy underbrush and try and jump the machine guns from the rear. He didn't know how many of them there were. He didn't know for sure where they were hid. But he figured it was the only chance. So three squads of us done dropped back and made our way around on the left.

Sergeant Bernard Early was in charge and Corporal Murray Savage and Corporal William Cutting and myself each led our squads. The privates under us were:

Dymowski
Weiler
Waring
Wins
Swanson
Muzzi
Beardsley
Konotski
Sok
Johnson
Saccina
Donohue
Wills

So you see there were just seventeen of us Boys went around on the left flank to see if we couldnt put those guns out of action.

According to orders, we got around on the left and in single file advanced forward through the brush towards where we could hear the machine-gun fire. We, done went very quietly and quickly. We had to. We kept well to the left and deep in the brush. At first we didn't see any Germans and we were not under heavy fire. Jes a few stray bullets. Without any loss and in right-smart time we done skirted the left side of the valley and were over on the hill somewhere near where the German machine guns were placed. The heavy brush and the hilly nature of the country hid us from the enemy. We were now nearly three hundred yards to the left and in front of our own front line. When we figured that we were right on the ridge that the Germans were on, we done stopped for a minute and had a little conference. Some of the boys wanted to attack from the flank. But Early and me and some of the others thought it would be best to keep on going until we were well behind the German lines, and then suddenly swing in and try and jump them from the rear. We done decided to try and do this. We opened up in skirmishing order and sorter flitted from brush to brush, using all the cover we could and pushing on as fast as possible. We had now sorter encircled the German left end and were going away in deep behind them without them knowing anything about it.

So when we went a round and fell in Behind those guns we first seen to germans with a Red Cross Band on their arm. So we ask them to stop and they did not so some one of the Boys shot at them and they run Back to our right. So we all run after them. They jumped out of the brush in front of us and run like two scared rabbits. We called to them to surrender, and one of our boys done fired and missed. And they kept on a-going. And we kept on after them. We wanted to capture them before they gave the alarm. We now knowed by the sounds of the firing that we were somewhere behind the German trench and in the rear of the machine guns that were holding up our big advance. We still couldn't see the Germans and they couldn't see us. But we could hear them machine guns shooting something awful. Savage's squad was leading, then mine, and then Cutting's. Sergeant Early was out in front, leading the way. We then jumped across a little stream of water that was there they was a Bout 15 or 20 Germans jumped up and throwed up their hands and said Comrade So the one in charge of us Boys told us not to shoot they was going to give up any way.

It was headquarters. There were orderlies, stretcher bearers, runners, a major and two officers sitting or standing around a sort of small wooden shack. They seemed to be having a sort of conference. And they done jes had breakfast too. And there was a mess of beefsteaks, jellies, jams, and loaf bread around. They were unarmed. All except the major. And some of them were in their shirt sleeves. By the way they were going on we knowed they never even dreamed that there were any Americans near them.

Germans caught totally off guard as
York and his patrol snuck behind two German lines

Of course, we were most as surprised as they were, coming on them so sudden. But we kept our heads and jumped them right smart, and covered them and told them to put up their hands and to keep them up. And they done done it. And we fired a few shots just to sorter impress them. I guess they thought the whole American Army was in their rear. And we didn't stop to tell them any different. Sergeant Early, who was in command of us, told us to hold our fire, as we had them, but to keep them covered and to hurry up and search and line them up. just as he was turning around from giving this order and we were moving forward to obey, some machine guns up on the hill in front of us and between us and the American lines, suddenly turned around and opened fire on us.

By the time Americans arrived overseas, the Germans were crack shots with their machine guns. They could hit lemons at 100 yds.

Sergeant Early went down with five bullets through the lower part of his body and one through his arm. Corporal Savage was killed. He must have had over a hundred bullets in his body. His clothes were 'most all shot off. And Corporal Cutting was also all shot up. Six of the other boys were killed or wounded. That machine-gun burst came sorter sudden and unexpected. And it done got us hard. The moment it begun the German prisoners fell flat on their faces. So did the rest of us American boys who were still standing. You see, while we, were capturing headquarters the German machine gunners up there on the hill seed us and done turned their guns around and let us have it.

After the first few bursts a whole heap of other machine guns joined in. There must have been over twenty of them and they kept up a continuous fire. Never letting up. Thousands of bullets kicked up the dust all around us. The undergrowth was cut down like as though they used a scythe. The air was just plumb full of death. Some of our boys done huddled up against the prisoners and so were able to get some protection and at the same time guard the prisoners. Some others crawled under cover, or jumped up and got behind trees. I was caught out in the open, a little bit to the left and in front of the group of prisoners and about twenty-five yards away from the machine guns which were in gun pits and trenches upon the hillside above me. I was now in charge.

York moved into position and opened fire all by himself.

By this time some of the Germans from on the hill was shooting at us. Well I was giving them the Best I had, and by this time the Germans had got their machine guns turned around and fired on us so they killed 6 and wounded 3. So that just left 8 and then we got into it right By this time So we had a hard Battle for a little while. I hadn't time to give no orders nohow. There was such a noise and racket all around that I would not have been heard even if I had done given them. I had no time nohow to do nothing but watch them there German machine gunners and give them the best I had. Every time I seed a German I jes teched him off. At first I was shooting from a prone position; that is lying down; jes like we often shoot at the targets in the shooting matches in the mountains of Tennessee; and it was jes about the same distance. But the targets here were bigger. I jes couldn't miss a German's head or body at that distance. And I didn't. Besides, it weren't no time to miss nohow. I knowed that in order to shoot me the Germans would have to get their heads up to see where I was lying. And I knowed that my only chance was to keep their heads down. And I done done it. I covered their positions and let fly every time I seed anything to shoot at. Every time a head come up I done knocked it down.

Then they would sorter stop for a moment and then another head would come up and I would knock it down, too. I was giving them the best I had. I was right out in the open and the machine guns were spitting fire and cutting up all around me something awful. But they didn't seem to be able to hit me. All the time the Germans were shouting orders. You never heard such a racket in all of your life. I still hadn't time or a chance to look around for the other boys. I didn't know where they were now. I didn't know what they were doing. I didn't even know if they were still living. Later on they done said that in the thick of the fight they didn't fire a shot.

Of course, all of this only took a few minutes. As soon as I was able I stood up and begun to shoot offhand, which is my favourite position. I was still sharpshooting with that-there old army rifle. I used up several clips. The barrel was getting hot and my rifle ammunition was running low, or was where it was hard for me to get at it quickly. But I had to keep on shooting jes the same.

In the middle of the fight a German officer and five men done jumped out of a trench and charged me with fixed bayonets. They had about twenty-five yards to come and they were coming right smart. I only had about half a clip left in my rifle; but I had my pistol ready. I done flipped it out fast and teched them off, too.

I teched off the sixth man first; then the fifth; then the fourth; then the third; and so on. That's the way we shoot wild-turkeys at home. You see we don't want the front ones to know that we're getting the back ones, and then they keep on coming until we get them all. Of course, I hadn't time to think of that. I guess I jes naturally did it. I knowed, too, that if the front ones wavered, or if I stopped them the rear ones would drop down and pump a volley into me and get me.

Then I returned to the rifle, and kept right on after those machine guns. I knowed now that if I done kept my head and didn't run out of ammunition I had them. So I done hollered to them to come down and give up. I didn't want to kill any more'n I had to. I woud tech a, couple of them off and holler again.

But I guess they couldn't understand my language, or else they couldn't hear me in the awful racket that was going on all around. Over twenty Germans were killed by this time. I got hold of a german magor and he told me if I wouldn't kill any more of them he would make them quit firing. So I told him alright if he would do it now. so he blew a little whistle and they quit shooting and come down and give up.

I think he had done been firing at me while I was fighting the machine guns—I examined his pistol later and sure enough hit was empty. Jes the same, he hadn't pestered me nohow. After he seed me stop the six Germans who charged with fixed bayonets he got up off the ground and walked over to me and yelled "English?"

I said, “No, not English.”

He said, “What?”

I said, “American.”

He said, “Good Lord!” Then he said, “If you won’t shoot any more I will make them give up.”

I told him he had better. I covered him with my automatic and told him if he didn’t make them stop firing I would take his head next. And he knowed I meaned it. So he blowed a little whistle and they come down out of the trench and throwed down their guns and equipment and held up their hands and begun to gather around. I guess, though, one of them thought he could get me. He had his hands up all right. But he done had a little hand grenade concealed, and as he come up to me he throwed it right at my head. But it missed me and wounded one of the prisoners. I hed to tech him off. The rest surrendered without any more trouble. There must have been about fifty of them.

We ended up with about 80 or 90 Germans there disarmed and had another line of Germans to go through to get out. So I called for my men and one of them answered from behind a big oak tree and the others were on my right in the brush so I said lets get these germans out of here. So one of my men said it is impossible so I said no lets get them out. So when my men said that this german magor said how many have you got and I said I have got a plenty and pointed my pistol at him all the time-in this battle I was using a rifle or a 45 Colts automatic pistol. So I lined the germans up in a line of twos and got between the ones in front and I had the german magor before me. So I marched them straight into those other machine guns and I got them.

The Germans were lined up two by two with Americans in the center for protection.

The German major could speak English as well as I could. Before the war he used to work in Chicago. When the prisoners in the first trench surrendered I Yelled out to my to let's get them out. And one of my men said it was impossible to get so many prisoners back to the American lines. And I told him to shut up and to let's get them out. Then the German major became suspicious and wanted to know how many men I had. And I told him I had a-plenty. And I told him to keep his hands up and to line up his men in a column of two and to do it in double time. And he did it. And I lined up my men that were left on either side of the column and I told one to guard the rear.

Sergeant Early and Corporal Cutting then come up towards me. Corporal Cutting said: "I am hit and hit bad." He was wounded in the arm. He done had all the buttons shot off his uniform and there was a great big "X" shot in his helmet. Sergeant Early said: "York, I am shot and shot bad. What shall I do?" I knowed by the look of him that he was very badly-wounded. He was dazed and in most awful pain. I done told them they could come out in the rear of our column with the other boys.

I ordered the prisoners to pick up and carry our wounded. I wasn't a-goin' to leave any good American boys lying out there to die. So I made the Germans carry them. And they did. And I takened the major and placed him at the head of the column and I got behind him and used him as a screen. I poked back and told him to hike. And he hiked. I guess I had him bluffed. It was pretty hard to tell in the brush and with all the noise and confusion around which way to go. The major done suggested we go down the gully. Then I knowed that was the wrong way. And I told him we were not going down any gully. We were going straight through the German front-line trenches back to the American lines. It was their second line that I had captured. We sure did get a long way behind the German trenches. And so I done marched them straight at that old German front-line trench. And some more machine guns swung around to fire. I told the major to blow his whistle or I would take his head and theirs too. So he blowed his whistle and they all done surrendered. All except one. I made the major order him to surrender twice. But he wouldn't. And I had to tech him off. I hated to do it. I've been doing a tol'able lot of thinking about it since. He was probably a brave soldier boy. But I couldn't afford to take any chance, and so I had to let him have it. There was considerably over a hundred prisoners now. It was a problem to get them back safely to our own lines. There was so many of them there was danger of our own artillery mistaking us for a German counter-attack and opening up on us. I sure was relieved when we run into the relief squads that had been sent forward through the brush to help us.

So when I got back to my magors P.C. (Patrol Camp). I had 132 prisoners. We marched those German prisoners on back into the American lines to the Battalion P. C. and there we come to the Intelligence Department and Lieutenant Woods come out and counted them and counted 132. We were ordered to take them out to Regimental Headquarters at Chatel Chehery; and from there all the way back to Division Headquarters and turn them over to the Military Police. We had such a mess of German prisoners that nobody seemed to want to take them over. So we had to take them back a right-far piece ourselves.

American field prisions like this held hundreds of captured German prisoners.The prisioners were treated humanely.

On the way back we were constantly under heavy shell fire and I had to double-time them to get them through safely. There was nothing to be gained by having any more of them wounded or killed. They done surrendered to me and it was up to me to look after them. And so I done done it. I had orders to report to Brigadier General Lindsay, our brigadier commander, and he said to me, "Well, York, I hear you have captured the whole German army." And I told him I only had 132

I didn't want to kill a whole heap of Germans nohow. I didn't hate them. But I done it jes the same. I had to. I was cornered. It was either them or me, and I'm a-telling you I didn't and don't want to die nohow if I can live. If they done surrendered as I wanted them to when I hollered to them first, and kept on hollering to them, I would have given them the protection that I give them later when I tuk them back. But they wouldn't surrender, and there was no way out for me but to tech them off.

Jes the same I have tried to forget. I have never talked about it much. I have never told the story even to my own mother. For years I done refused to write about it for the newspapers, and wasn't at all pleased when others wrote about it.

But now that the story is coming out I want it to come out right, and I want everything brought out. Everything. There were others in that fight besides me. Some of them, Sergeant Early for instance, and others too, played a right-smart part in things until they were shot down. I'm a-telling you they're entitled to a whole heap of credit. It isn't for me, of course, to decide how much credit they should get. But jes the same, I'm a-telling you a heap of those boys were heroes and America ought to be proud of them.

So, I'm a-going to publish the documents and I'm a-going to do it right here. They speak for themselves.

I might add that if there are any differences in them it is kinder well to remember that no two people ever see the same thing alike. It is also true that people who are not trained to write down what they have seed and been through and most of them-there boys were not trained that way ain't always in agreement when they write about the same thing. Jes the same, the documents give a right-smart account of the goings-on in the forest that awful morning.

CHAPTER 25

THE OFFICIAL STORY

Most all of the documents are copied from the originals in the War Department in Washington, or in the possession of Major George Edward Buxton, Jr., the official historian of the Eighty-second Division. These reports had to be made before Alvin York could receive his Congressional Medal of Honor, America's highest military award.

York writes:

The complete official record of the story has to include one more document. My own account as it was takened down at Divisional Headquarters a short time after the fight. I don't much care to publish the first part of it. But it is a part of the document and is an exact copy of the original, which is in the War Department in Washington, and I ain't got no right to leave any of it out. I have to publish it all or not at all. So I have no choice but to put it all in. I might say that this is the first time that this document has ever been published.

York explained his feat using a field map such as this one.

Official report

The records of the 82d Division reveal no more extraordinary act of individual gallantry and achievement than is accredited, after careful investigation, to Sergeant Alvin C. (No. 1,910,426) York, Co. G, 328thInfantry. York is a farmer, 31 years old, whose home is located at Pall Mall, Tenn., in the mountainous and northeastern corner of the state.

On the 8th of October, 1918, York was a corporal in G Company, 328th Infantry. This company was the left assault company of the 2d Battalion, which jumped off from the crest of Hill 223 just north of Chatel Chehery and attacked due west, with its objective, the Decauville Railroad, two kilometres due west. The success of this assault had a far-reaching effect in relieving the enemy pressure against American forces in the heart of the Argonne Forest. The local success achieved by this battalion was, in itself, of outstanding proportions. About 300 prisoners were taken and nearly 200 dead Germans left on the ground and material captured which included four 77s, a trench mortar battery, a complete signal outfit and 123 machine guns. The attack was driven through in spite of resistance of a very savage character and most destructive enemy machine gun and artillery fire. The battalion suffered enfilade fire from both flanks.

The part which Corporal York individually played in this attack is difficult to fully estimate. Practically unassisted, he captured 132 Germans (three of whom were officers), took about 35 machine guns and killed no less than 25 of the enemy, later found by others on the scene of York's extraordinary exploit. York is well known in his section of Tennessee for his remarkable skill with both rifle and pistol.

The following story has been carefully checked in every possible detail from headquarters of this division and is entirely substantiated.

Although Sergeant York's statement tends to underestimate the desperate odds which he overcame, it has been decided to forward to higher authority the account given in his own words:

"Sergeant Harry M. Parsons was in command of a platoon of which my, squad was a part. This platoon was left support platoon of G Company, my squad forming the extreme left flank of the platoon. The valley was covered by machine-gun fire from the right [pointing at the map], from the front, and from the left front. Machine guns from the left front were causing a great deal of damage to our troops advancing across the valley. Sergeant Parsons was ordered to advance with his platoon and cover our left flank. As the fire was very hot in the valley, we decided to skirt the foot of the hill on our left and thereby gain some protection. We had advanced a little ways up to about here [pointing at the map] when we were held up, by machine guns from our left front here [pointing at the map]. Sergeant Parsons told Sergeant Bernard Early to take two squads and put these machine guns out of business, my squad, being the left squad, was one of those chosen.

"We advanced in single file. The undergrowth and bushes here were so thick that we could see only a few yards ahead of us, but as we advanced, they became a little thinner. In order to avoid frontal fire from the machine guns, we turned our course slightly to the left, thereby working around on the right flank of the machine guns and somewhat to their rear, which caused us to miss these forward guns [pointing at the map]. As we gained a point about here [pointing at the map and designating a point somewhat in the rear of the machine guns], we turned sharply to the right oblique and followed a little path which took us directly in rear of the machine guns. As we advanced we saw two Boche with Red Cross bands on their arms. We called to them to halt, but they did not stop and we opened fire on them. Sergeant Early was leading and I was third.

"As I said before, we were proceeding in single file. We immediately dashed down a path, along which the Boche were running, and crossed this stream [pointing at map]. The Boche then turned to the right and ran in the direction from which we had come. When we reached the point where they turned, we stopped for half a second to form a skirmish line. I jumped about four paces away from a sergeant and we told the other men to scatter out because we thought there was going to be a battle and we did not want to be too close together. As soon as we formed our skirmish line we burst through the bushes after the Boche.

"This little stream of which I spoke runs through a gulch into the valley. On either side of the stream there was a little stretch of flat level ground, about twenty feet wide, which was covered with extremely thick bush. On the east bank of the stream was a hill having an exceedingly steep slope. This hill was some what semi-circular in shape and afforded excellent protection to anyone behind it. Along the top of the hill were the machine guns firing across the valley at our troops.

"We burst through the undergrowth and were upon the Germans before we knew it, because the undergrowth was so thick that we could see only a few yards ahead of us. There was a little shack thrown together that seemed to be used as a sort of a P. C. by the Germans. In front of this, in a sort of a semi-circular mass, sat about seventy-five Boche, and by the side of a chow can, which was near the P. C., sat the commanding officer and two other officers. The Bochc seemed to be having some kind of conference.

"When we burst in on the circle, some of the Boche jumped up and threw up their hands, shouting 'Kamerad.' Then the others jumped up, and we began shooting. About two or three Germans were hit. None of our men fell.

"Sergeant Early said: 'Don't shoot any more. They are going to give up anyhow,' and for a moment our fire ceased, except that one German continued to fire at me, and I shot him. In the meantime, the Boche upon the hill with the machine guns swung the left guns to the left oblique and opened fire on us. I was at this time just a few paces from the mass of Boche who were crowded around the P. C. At first burst of fire from the machine guns, all the Boche in this group hit the ground, lying flat on their stomachs. I, and a few other of our men, hit the ground at the same time. Those who did not take cover were either killed or wounded by the Boche machine-gun fire, the range being so close that the clothes were literally torn from their bodies. Sergeant Early and Corporal Cutting were wounded, and Corporal Savage was killed. In this first fire we had six killed and three wounded. By this time, those of my men who were left had gotten behind trees, and two men sniped at the Boche. They fired about half a clip each. But there wasn't any tree for me, so I just sat in the mud and used my rifle, shooting at the Boche machine gunners. I am a pretty good shot with the rifle, also with the pistol, having used them practically all my life, and having had a great deal of practice. I shot my rifle until I did not have any more dips convenient and then I used my pistol.

"The Boche machine-gun fire was sweeping over the mass of Germans who were lying flat, and passing a few inches over my head, but I was so close to the mass of Germans who were lying down that the Boche machine gunners could not hit me without hitting their own men. There were about fifty Boche with the machine guns and they were under the command of a lieutenant. By this time, the remaining Boche guns had been turned around and were firing at us, and the lieutenant with eight or ten Germans armed with rifles rushed toward us. One threw a little grenade, about the size of a dollar and with a string that you pull like this when you want to explode it, at me, but missed me by a few feet, wounding, however, one of his own men.

"I just let the Boche come down the hill and then poured it into them with my pistol, and I am, as I said before, a pretty good shot with the pistol. I shot the lieutenant, and when he was killed the machine-gun fire ceased. During the fight, I kept hearing a pistol firing from the midst of the Boche who were lying on the ground. This was evidently the commanding officer shooting, as he was the only one in the crowd armed with a pistol, and all of his dips were empty when I examined them later.

"When the machine guns ceased firing the commanding officer, who spoke English, got off the ground and walked over to me. He said: 'English?' I said: 'No, not English.' He said: 'What?' I said: 'American.' He said: 'Good Lord.' Then he said: 'If you won't shoot any more, I will make them give up,' and I said: 'Well, all right, I will treat you like a man,' and he turned around and said something to his men in German, and they all threw off their belts and arms and the machine gunners threw down their arms and came down the hill.

"I called to my men and one of them answered me from over here, another from over here, and another here (they were pretty well scattered), and when they all come to me, I found that there were six left besides myself.

"We searched the Boche and told them to line up in a column of twos. The Boche commanding officer wanted to line up facing north and go down through the valley along the road which runs by the foot of the hill, but I knew if they got me there it would be as good as they wanted on account of the machine guns on the opposite slope, so I said, 'No, I am going this way,' which was the way I had come, and which led through the group of machine guns placed here [pointing at the map], which seemed to be outpost guns. We had missed this machine-gun nest as we advanced, because we had gone further to the left.

"When we got the Boche lined up in a column of twos, I scattered my men along and at the rear of the column and told them to stay well to the rear and that I would lead the way. So I took the commanding officer and the two other officers and put one in front of me and one on each side of me, and we headed the column. I did that because I knew that if I were caught on the side of the column, the machine gunners would shoot me, but that if I kept in the column, they would have to shoot their officers before they could kill me. In this manner we advanced along a path and into the machine-gun nest which is situated here [pointing at the map].

"The machine gunners, as I said before, could not kill me without killing their officers, and I was ready for them. One aimed a rifle at me from behind a tree, and, as I pointed my pistol at him, the commanding officer said: 'If you won't shoot any more, I will tell them to surrender.' He did and we added them to our column.

"I then reported with the prisoners to the Battalion P. C. They were counted there and there were 132 of them. I was there ordered to deliver the prisoners to Brigade Headquarters, which I did, and returned to my company the next morning."

It is further interesting to note that Sergeant York was a member of the Church of Christ in Christian Union. During the training days at Camp Gordon, Atlanta, Ga., he informed his company commander of his church affiliations, and was seriously troubled by the fact that one of the fundamental tenets of this faith is a pronounced opposition to war. This continued to cause York the most genuine perplexity, although he carefully refrained from accepting the military status of conscientious objector, declaring that he proposed to obey all orders while a member of the Army. His mental doubts were finally dissipated by his company commander in a long interview before embarking at Camp Upton, N. Y., at the end of which York stated that the purposes of American participation were of such a character that he felt himself able to take his part with a clear conscience.

Supplementary statement by Sergeant Alvin C. York, Company G, 328th Infantry:

"After the German captain had made the Germans remaining on the hill surrender and the firing stopped, Corporals Early and Cutting came up toward me. Corporal Cutting said: "I'm hit and hit bad,' and Corporal Early said: 'York, I am 'shot, and shot bad. What shall I do?' I told him: 'You can come out in the rear of our column with the other boys.' Private Donohue helped Corporal Early out to the edge of the Woods, where they met a stretcher bearer from G Company with a stretcher, and Corporal Early was carried back to Chatel, Cheherry, when the German prisoners carried him to the ambulance. Corporal Early was shot through the lower body. Corporal Cutting was shot three times in the left arm. Private Muzzi was shot in the shoulder. Corporal Cutting and Private Muzzi walked out themselves. No German wounded, as far as any of us know, came out with our prisoners. The wounded German lieutenant was brought out, I think, afterwards by German prisoners who went back for him. When we got back to the Battalion P. C., the prisoners were counted by Lieutenant Woods and Lieutenant Garner. Lieutenant Woods told us to take them to the Battalion P. C. and Colonel Wetherill told us to take them to Brigade Headquarters at Varennes. Another group of prisoners were added to those we had and I turned over at Varennes 208 prisoners to the Military Police, and a receipt was given to Corporal Clark, who had joined us after the fight was over. The prisoners which were captured and which were counted at the Battalion P. C. by Lieutenants Woods and Garner, I am told, amounted to 132. I counted them roughly by myself and thought there were about 146."

Here is the official list of the men participating in action of October 8th, 1919, capturing 132 prisoners.

KILLED

Corp. Murray Savage
Pvt. Maryan E. Dymowski
Pvt. Ralph E. Weiler
Pvt. Fred Warning
Pvt. William Wins
Pvt Walter E. Swanson

WOUNDED

Sgt. Bernard Early

Corp. William S. Cutting
Pvt. Marie Muzzi

SURVIVORS
Crop. Alvin C. York
Pvt. Percy Beardsley
Pvt. Joe Konotski
Pvt. Feodor Sok
Pvt. Thos. C. Johnson
Pvt. Michael A. Saccina
Pvt. Patrick Donohue
Pvt. George Wills

Official picture taken just after the battle on the spot where the action took place.

CHAPTER 26

AFTER THE SMOKE HAS CLEARED

About ten o'clock on the morning of October 9th, I reported to Captain Danforth at the railroad. On account of the long distance we had to go back from where we handed over the prisoners and the most awful rough nature of the country and the mix-up and confusion everywhere, it takened me 'most all night to get back to him again. The company done been all mussed up and there were only a few left, but they kept on a-going through everything, and they done busted that old railroad. The Captain asked me where I had been. I told him of the fight with the machine guns around on the left flank; of how the other non-commissioned officers had been killed or wounded; and how I had takened command and marched them prisoners away back behind the lines to Divisional Headquarters. He asked me why I hadn't handed them over at Battalion Headquarters and then pushed on and joined him. I told him that there was a whole heap of prisoners and nobody would take them from me and I had to take them all the way back. He asked me how many prisoners there were and when I told him one hundred and thirty-two, he looked at me with a funny-like expression in his face. He seemed kinder surprised.

I had been away from Captain Danforth and the company for over twenty-four hours, and I knowed he needed me most awful bad now. He needed every man he could get, because there was only a few left. Jes the same I had been doing a heap of thinking about the boys we had left behind in the fight. There was jes a chance that some of them might be only wounded and still lying out there in pain and needing help some thing terrible. I felt I jes had to go and look for them. So I asked the Captain if I couldn't take some stretcher bearers and orderlies and go back and look around, and though he needed me most awful bad he said it was all right, I could get the detail and go back.

Dead and wounded were often carried out.

So I got me two stretcher bearers and led them back to the place where I done fought the German machine guns. When we got there the Salvage Corps had already done come and cleaned up the place; they packed up the equipment and takened it away. And they done buried the dead, our own boys, and the Germans. The ground there all around looked like the most torndowndest place I ever had seen. There was an old canteen lying within a few inches of where I stood. It had eighteen bullet holes in it. There was a shrapnel helmet a couple of feet away, and it was all sorter sieved, jes like the top of a pepper box. The ground in front and on both sides of where we done stood was all soft and torned up with bullets. The brush on either side was also torned up and there was a sort of tunnel cut in the brush behind me. Everything destroyed, torned up, killed—trees, grass, men. Oh, my, it was a terrible sight. But we didn't find no wounded nowhere. We not only searched with our eyes, we searched with our voices. We yelled, thinking that maybe someone was in the bushes. But no one yelled back.

There weren't no wounded that we could see; neither American nor German. There weren't no bodies around neither. All was terribly quiet in the field. And I jes couldn't help thinking of the boys that only the day before was alive and like me. Dymowski—dead. Weiler—dead. Waring—dead. Wins—dead. Swanson—dead. Corporal Murray Savage, my best pal, dead. Oh, my, it seemed so unbelievable. I would never see them again. I would never share the same blanket with Corporal Savage. We'd never read the Bible together again. We would never talk about our faith and pray to our God. I was mussed up inside worsen than I had ever been. I'm a-telling you when you lose your best buddie and you know you ain't never going to see him again, you sorter know how terrible cruel war is. There was nothing I could do now for Corporal Murray Savage or any of the other boys that done lost their lives. I could only pray for their souls. And I done that. I prayed for the Greeks and Italians and the Poles and the Jews and the others. I done prayed for the Germans too. They were all brother men of mine. Maybe their religion was different, but I reckon we all believed in the same God and I wanted to pray for all of them.

So we went back, and I remember the boys that got wounded, and was a-hoping and praying they would get well. Early got five bullets in the body and one in the arm. And Cutting was bunged up right smart. His helmet was broken. The buttons were shot off'n his uniform, and he was hit in the arm. Well, I had come through it all without even a hair of my head being harmed. It seemed sorter hard to believe that I done come through alive. Two men on both sides of me and two others right behind me were killed, and I hadn't been touched. I triad to figure it out how it come that everybody around me who was exposed done got picked off or wounded and that I alone come out unharmed. I have been trying to figure it out ever since. And the more I figure the more I am convinced that it warsn't no mere luck or jes an accident. It must have been something more and bigger than that.

The officers and the experts who went over the battleground afterwards, some of them several times, and who takened the statements of all of us who came through the fight, have tried to give their own explanations of how I come through.

Some of them say that for fear of hittin' their own men who were prisoners the German machine gunners had to raise their fire and shoot high, and so the bullets done passed just a few inches over my head. I'm admittin' that that's a right-smart lot of reasonin', but jes the same they didn't fire too high when they opened on us. They hit a whole heap of other boys all around me. They cut up the ground at my feet when they riddled that old canteen and shrapnel helmet.

Others say that the German machine gunners were surprised and kinder rattled. They hadn't even dreamed that there were any Americans behind them or even near them. Then when we burst in on them they thought that we were the advance units of a big American attacking force which done either got in behind them or surrounded them. And that made them panicky. And they sorter got mixed up and didn't know what to do. I'm admittin' that that's good reasonin' too. There can be no doubt at all but what we did surprise them. We takened headquarters with only a few shots fired. But jes the same the German machine gunners were quick and were used to being in tight quarters. These were veteran troops that we done run into. They had been in the war a long time and done fought through many battles. They knowed what it was all about. Then there was so many of them and they had such a whole heap of machine guns that it don't stand to reason that they all sorter lost their nerve and give up. I can't admit that nohow. I know different. They fought like a heap of wild cats. I mean the machine gunners did. They kept up a continuous fire for several minutes. They killed and wounded a whole heap of our boys. They were surprised and some of them might have been panicky. But not all of them.

Some of the officers have sorter suggested that I was the 'right man in the right place.' They done tried to make the point that I was a right-smart sharpshooter; that I knowed how to handle weapons; that I could shoot equally well with rifle or pistol; that I could shoot from either hand, or from any position; and that this jes happened to be my favourite distance. They also claimed that I always was cool and deliberate under fire. I ain't so foolish as to deny that I know a whole heap about guns. I do. I know, too, that I am a tol'able good shot. But I don't care how good a shot man is, hit ain't in the nature of things for one man with an army rifle and a pistol to whip thirty-five machine guns that can each fire over six hundred shots a minute; from a p'int-blank range of between twenty and thirty yards.

Some of them officers have been saying that I being a mountain boy and accustomed to woods and nature done all these things the right way jes by instinct, like an animal when it is cornered. There may be something in that. I hain't never got much larnin' from books, except the Bible. Maybe my instincts is more natural than of men who ain't been brunged up like I was in the woods and in the mountains. But that ain't enough to account for the way I come out alive, with all those German soldiers and machine guns raining death on me.

I am willing to admit that all of these explanations have a whole heap of truth in them. I am willing to admit that maybe I had all the breaks, and had them right. Jes the same, there was something else. There had to be something more than man power in that fight to save me. There can't no man in the world make me believe there weren't. And I'm a-telling you the hand of God must have been in that fight. It surely must have, been divine power that brought me out. No other power under heaven could save a man in a place like that. Men were killed on both sides of me and all around me and I was the biggest and the most exposed of all. Jes think of them thirty machine guns raining fire on me p'int-blank from a range of only twenty-five yards and all of them-there rifles and pistols besides, and those bombs, and then those men that charged with fixed bayonets, and I never receiving a scratch, and bringing in one hundred and thirty-two prisoners. I have got only one explanation to offer, and only one: without the help of God I jes couldn't have done it. There can be no arguments about that. I am not going to believe different as long as I live. I'm a-telling you that God must have heard my prayers long before I done started for France. I'm a-telling you He done give me my assurance that so long as I believed in Him He would protect me. That's why when I bade my mother and Gracie and all my brothers and sisters and Rosier Pile good-bye before sailing for France I told them all not to worry, I would be safe, I would come back.

I done settled it all with my God long ago before I went overseas. I done prayed and prayed to Him; He done given me my assurance that so long as I believed in Him He would protect me, and He did.

So you can see here in this case of mine where God helped me out. I had been living for God and working in the church work sometime before I come to the army. So I am a witness to the fact that God did help me out of that hard battle; for the bushes were shot off all around me and I never got a scratch. So you can see that God will be with you if you will only trust him and I say that He did save me———

Now He will save you if you will only trust Him.

CHAPTER 27

The Armistice

But the fightin' hadn't done stopped yet. There was some more big battles ahead, terrible battles. And I was only wishing and praying that a good God would bring all this man-killing desolation to an end.

October 9th Argonne Forest.

Well now as we went on fighting our way through the thick forest of the Argonne woods we could hear the cryes of our boys who were getting shot and oh my we had to sleep by the dead and with the dead. But when we were seeing so many of our boys being shot all we could say is just to say as we seen our fallen Comrades Good by pal; I don't know where you is camping now:

Whether you've pitched your tent 'neath azure skies;
Or whether o'er your head the bleak storm winds blow
I only know that when your final call come for you
It almost broke my heart to see you go.

But I trust pal that you was ready to meet that last call. Yes, and now you be carefull that the last final call don't find you not ready to meet your God in peace.

October 12th
Somerance, Argonne Forest

We had got to Somerance and during this time we had lost heavy on our men and was still losing them as you know that you cant fight in war without losing men and the Germans was shelling us awfull with big shells also gas and the boys laying there that they couldn't burry. Oh my I cant tell you how I felt and when those big shells would come over and burst then I heard my comrades crying and mourning. All we could do was to trust God to protect us and look up and say:

Good by old pal, Your body sleeps beer 'neath the sod, Your soul I pray has gone home to God.

But yet I cant know the greenwood tree that leads into the vale beyond. Not yet. So close by this pal, my solitary bunk I had to make to stay over night and oh how lonely how sad no tongue can tell. But yet God was with me. Is God with you if not please don't do as many others have done Put it off to long.

So we stayed in the front at Somerance untill we git releaved by the 80th Div. boys.

We stayed in actual fighting in the Argonne from the time we went in, which was the morning of October 8th to November 1st. Over three weeks. Fighting in the front line all the time and through those terrible woods. And we were both mussed up right smart. The woods and us. Those old woods were all ruined. And we were all shot to pieces. There were not many of them-there Greeks and Italians left. But what was left were still fighting like a sackful of wildcats. I shore did like those boys now. They were my buddies. Yes; they were still burning up a most awful amount of ammunition. But they always kept on a-going. Always. The nearest I come to getting killed in France was in an apple orchard in Somerance in the Argonne. It was several days after the fight with the machine guns. We hed a very heavy barrage from the Germans suddenly drop down on us, and we were ordered to dig in and to lose no time about it. Some of us were digging in under an apple tree. The shells were bursting purty close. But we didn't take much notice of them. Jes kept right on a-digging. It's funny, after you've been at the front a right-smart while you can almost tell where the shells are going to burst and what size they are. It is a sort of Soldier's instinct. And this morning they were close, but not close enough to scare us. And then they got closer. And we dug faster. I have dug on farms and in gardens and in road work and on railroad, but it takes big shells dropping close to make you really dig. And I'm a-telling you, the dirt was flying. And then bang!ss one of the big shells struck the ground right in front of us and we all went up in the air. But we all come down again. Nobody was hurt. But it sure was close.

"The shells were bursting purty close. But we didn't take much notice of them. Jes kept right on a-digging." (But for the providence of God, York would have been blown to pieces right after his famed battle.)

November 1, 1918
Argonne Forest

So we came out of the lines to a germans rest camp and there we got something to eat. I was made a sergeant just as quick as I got back out of the lines. But, oh, my ! so many of my old buddies were missing and we scarcely seemed the same outfit. And then we started out and hiked to a French camp. (No place given). We loaded on French busses to go to another French Camp. On November 5th we arrived to a French camp. On the 7th I taken a train for Aix-les-Bain. I had a furlough for 10 days.

November 8-10, 1918
Aix-les-Bain

So I got to Aix-les-Bain and went to the Hotel de Albion and I stayed at this hotel from the 8th to the 16th and I went a round and seen some fine scenery I got on a motor boat and went over to Itala and there I seen some good scenery.

There was a bunch of us had been given a ten-day leave to Aix-les-Bains. We went down there for a rest. We had several weeks without any relief and were tired and worn out and went down there to rest during the ten-day leave. We were staying in private places. We jes went around seeing the historical places, the old Roman baths and up on the mountain.

I went to church. I think the man gave us a very good talk his subject was the angle [angel] helping the wounded to the aid station. And there I also seen the old Roman baths that they said was built 122 years before Christ. And then it all come to an end. All of this killing and destroying.

November 11, 1918
Aix-les-Bain

Marshal Foch and the train car where the Armistice was signed.

The Amistice was signed. And they sure was a time in that city that day and night. Yes. say did you think that the armistice was sign on 11th month on the 11th day and the 11th hour of 1918. And a nother thing did you ever know that the war just lasted 585 days from the time that the President declared war against Germany until the armistice was signed and did you ever know that in this little short time of 585 days that the Americans was over here in France a holding a 77 mile frount in the Argonne forest.

I don't know that I can jes exactly tell my feelings at that time. It was awful noisy, all the French were drunk, whooping and hollering. The Americans were drinking with them, all of them. I never done anything much. Jes went to church and wrote home and read a little. I did not go out that night. I had jes gotten back there and were all tired. I was glad the armistice was signed, glad it were all over. There had been enough fighting and killing. And my feelings were like most all of the American boys. It was all over. And we were ready to go home. I felt that they had done the thing they should have done, signing the armistice.

York spent celebrating the end of the war in church.

CHAPTER 28

The Celebration

Americans in the field celebrated to hear that the War had come to an end.

The rejoicings which followed the armistice lasted for several days. I didn't take no part in them. I don't know why. I kinder think I felt it all so much that I daresn't let myself go.

On November 17, I stopped at Champlitte, France, and the French had a dance that night and they had to go by my bed to where they was dancing and the girls would pull my feet until I couldn't sleep for them pestering me.

December 25, 1918
Long, France

I went to see President Wilson and wife at Long, where they had a review. So there was a large crowd there. I enjoyed myself very well But I didn't get any dinner So I was not enjoying a Christmas dinner you see, Ho! Ho! So I went back to my company that night and it was after dark. So Mrs. Wilson was dressed very nice and she had a smile on her face all the time. She was wearing a Smart Seal Skin Coat with a Big Fox Collar and a close fitting Seal Skin Toque with a bright red rose trimming on one side and a little bunch of holly at her throat. So she looked very pleasing and Mr. Wilson was wearing a large black silk hat with a light grey fur coat he also had a smile on his face So that cheered the boys to see Mr. and Mrs. Wilson and hear them talk, Ho! Ho!

York shared his story to troops throughout France.

In January I begun to travel over France and talk to the boys. I was travelling in and out of my Division Headquarters something like six weeks. I travelled by motor cycle and automobile. I would jes go to a place and the boys would come around and I would hold a meeting and talk to them. I spoke in the Y huts and out in the open to the battalions and to the assembled troops on the ground. I got good representation everywhere. Our division chaplain, Rev. C. Tyler, of Milwaukee, often travelled with me. He was a nice man and a powerful preacher. I first talked to the boys in our Eighty-second Division and then I went to other outfits.

On one of these trips they done drove me about eighty miles an hour on a motor cycle over those old French roads. It was asking too much of God, travelling like that. In front of the machine guns in the Argonne I couldn't protect myself. So I expected Him to look after me. And He done it and I come out unharmed. But there was no sense rushing like mad over those old roads on a motor cycle. So I wouldn't do it.

The boys were longing to get home. They felt they had done their jobs. The war was over. They were kinder restless. I was that way too. Now that there was nothing much to do I begun to get homesick again. I begun to think more and more of the log cabin in the Valley of the Three Forks of the Wolf at home in Tennessee, and of my little old mother, and of Gracie.

Oh, my! How slow those cold wet days in camp went by. There was nothing to do and so much time to do it in. I don't like fooling around like that nohow. I kinder think the waiting, waiting, waiting pestered me a heap more than the war itself did. It jes seemed as though that old ship to take us home would never come.

February 12-26th 1918
Prauthoy, France

I sit a Round all day didnt do anything. It was so cold and snowy that I never did anything but sit by the fire. I went to church. It was Sunday and a rainy day, and we had a nice walk. I never done anything much for I was not feeling good.

On the night of the 26th of February I taken the a vant and started for Bordeaux. En Route to Bordeaux. I was on the train and it came an awfull cold snow storm about 3 P.M. So we was in box-cars and it was cold and snowing and we had no fire. So it was pretty tough. But that was better than sleeping in those old French barnes where the cows sleep in the parlor and the chickens in the dining room.

It was even worse in Bordeaux. Jes cold, stormy days with nothing to do but sit around and think of home. Of course we did some drilling and marching. And there were guards and reviews which somehow now that the war was over didn't seem the same nohow. There was neither strength nor seasoning in them.

Once in a while though things did get a bit exciting. One night the officers had a dance in the Y hut. The privates were not allowed to go, but they done got tanked up on some of that-there French cognac. Then they sorter pushed in on the dance. They picked out most of the pretty girls; and the girls were kinder willing, too, Ho! Ho! And they sorter crowded the officers. I'm a-telling you that made them-there captains and lieutenants mad. They ordered me to call out the guard and get the boys off the floor. But that was a harder job than busting the Hindenburg Line. The boys hung on to the girls and didn't want to give them up or stop dancing nohow. The officers were just as determined to keep the dance private, that is for themselves and their girls. So I sorter arranged an armistice between them. I roped off that old dance floor and stationed the guards along the rope. So the officers were able to dance at one end. And the boys kept some of the girls and danced at the other end.

Later on in March I got me a leave pass and went to Paris. The first time, I didn't do much but hike round and see the sights. I done heard a lot about that-there opera. I had never heard of the word before. All I knowed about it from what the boys told me was that it was music, a lot of them stringed instruments playing together, so I hiked me to the place and bought a ticket and they done charged four dollars for a seat I sat through it all right. I liked the orchestra, but I don't think I'd ever again spend four dollars to see another opera like it. I went out to Versailles and wandered through the palaces there. I went to the tomb of Napoleon. I went to where they buried the unknown soldier but I didn't stay long because it sorter made me sad; and I didn't want to be sad in Paris; but I was sad jes the same. Of course I could have gone out like a whole heap of the boys and fooled around with the mademoiselles and the vin rouge; and sorter tried to forget the war and them there Germans I done killed in the Argonne. But I didn't drink and I had a girl of my own back home in the mountains. So I hiked around all day and at night time I jes got out in the streets and mixed in the crowd and then went home to bed.

York saw plenty of Paris Victory Parades.

I rode on the Paris wheel and took a train ride down to Se Louis 14 Plait at night. I kinder think that bestest of all I enjoyed my ride on the Paris wheel. I'm a-telling you that when it started to go round and round with me on it and the sky and the ground all got mixed up I not only forgot the war I done forgot everything, Ho! Ho!

I went back to Paris again in April. I was ordered to represent my division as a non-commissioned officer at the first meeting of the American Legion. That was when it was formed. I arrived in Paris at 8:30 A.M. and 10.30 A.M. was our meeting. I was there on time at the Hotel de Gabriel. So we had the meeting all day until 5:30 P.M. the meeting adjourned.

York spent his leisure time touring Paris,
although he longed for home.

So you see I'm a charter member of the American Legion. It begun right there in Paris, at the Hotel de Gabriel. The meeting lasted all day until about 5:30 in the afternoon. I attended all the sessions. I jes knowed hit was going to grow into a big organization. It sorter seemed right that the buddies who fought together in France should have some sort of organization that would keep them together in peace.

Once I got lost tramping round the streets. That is the only time that I ever got bewildered as to direction. Right in the middle of that-thar old city the streets are all sorter mixed up. They seem to have no beginnings and no ends. And when they do have ends they sorter go plumb up against a blank wall. They call it a cul-de-sac. So I got lost. I tried to get my direction by the sun, but I could not see it. Ho! Ho! I tried to remember some of the buildings. I couldn't. And I'm telling you I couldn't make heads nor tails out of the names of the streets. I didn't know where I was. All I knowed was I was in Paris. So I went up to a mademoiselle and I told her as well as I could that I was lost and would she be so kind as to tell me where my hotel was. She was a right-smart girl. She smiled and then takened me to a street car and put, me on it and told the mademoiselle conductor where I wanted to go and to let me off when I got there. She sure did too. So you see I never takened any girls home in France but one of them had to take me home, Ho! Ho!

One day some of us boys heard that the Queen of Roumania was coming in on the train, so we hiked down to the station. And sure enough she come and when she seed us she smiled and waved her hand. I was fairly close to her. She looked very pretty and she sorter walked like a queen. She had on a black dress and a kind of black veil.

I seed the Queen of Roumania. She is a very good-looking lady So I stayed in Paris until 8:26 on the night of the 9th.

I liked Paris all right. It was a right-smart city. Jes the same it sorter convinced me more than ever that cities don't mean much to me nohow. I knowed in my own heart that I wouldn't give up my mountains and the hunting and the shooting for all of the cities in the world. So soon as my leave was up I went back to the camp near Bordeaux. And I jes sat around there in the rain and the mud doing nothing and waiting for that-thar old ship to come and take us home. Oh, my! The days went by slower and slower. It jes seemed as if we would never get away from France. I'm a-telling you them were the homesickest days I ever had in my life.

At last we got ready to sail. The boat done came. I'm a-telling you I was tickled. So were the boys. But when we got down to the wharf and begun to load there were so many of us the boat wouldn't hold us all. And, oh, my I had to stay behind with sixty-six others and do some more waiting. That was pretty tough I'm a-telling you. But the next day another old boat came along and we done sailed jes the same.

CHAPTER 29

GOIN' HOME

May 10, 1918
Aboard the S.S. Ohioano

In the morning we went down to the docks and eat us a little and then we got on the S.S. Ohioan boat at 2:26 P.M. we broke loose from the shores of France and by dark we was out of sight of land.

We had about three or four days of storms and most awful rough seas. I was right-smart sick for several days. Had to stay down part of the time in my berth and part of the time on top of deck. I sure would have liked to see some trees or those old mountains. Oh, my, that sea I didn't feel like talking or doing anything but lying down and being left tol'ably alone. And then I knowed, too, that they were going to give me a big reception when I arrived in New York. They done wired out at sea. And that hed me worried. I would hev got out and walked if I could hev.

Sunday, May 18, 1918
At Sea

We had services in the afternoon. We Sing Jesus Saviour Pilot me and the reading was the first psam.

May 22, 1918
At Sea
Hoboken, N. J. At 2 P.M. I landed

York was just one of the smiling faces returning home.

The Tennessee society had a five-day furlough for me to see New York City. So I stopped at Waldorf Hotel.

Oh, my, I can't tell you how I felt when our ship steamed up New York Harbour and I seed the skyscrapers sorter standing up against the sky. In the distance they looked jes a little like the mountains at home when you see them from a long way off. Oh, my, I was so homesick I jes knowed I would never leave my country again. I didn't want to nohow. I stood there in the front of the ship as we steamed up the harbour and when we passed the Statue of Liberty I sorter looked her in the eyes and I kinder understood what the doughboy meant when he said: "Take a look at me, Old Girl. Take a good look at me, because whenever you want to see me again you will have to turn around."

I knowed, of course, that a committee from the Tennessee

Society was going to meet my boat. And they did. They tried to make a most awful fuss over me. They seemed to think I done done something wonderful. I couldn't see it that way nohow. I done done my duty like most any other soldier would have done when he was up against the same thing.

The Tennessee Society met me at the boat with a car. There was a right-smart heap of newspaper men there too and they made me stand around and have my picture taken. There were a whole heap of cameras. So you see I was under fire again. And they done questioned me. And by the time they had finished writing about me in their papers I had whipped the whole German Army single-handed. Ho, Ho. Those newspaper men! But they were very nice.

They gave me a right-smart reception in New York City. They drove me through the streets in an open car; and the streets were so crowded we could only go slow. It seemed as most everybody knowed me. They throwed a most awful lot of paper and ticker tape and confetti out of the windows of those big skyscrapers. I wondered what it was at first. It looked like a blizzard. I didn't understand that it was for me until they told me. I thought that they did the same thing for most every soldier that came back. I thought it was a New York habit. And a very nice habit, too.

York was overwhelmed with the celebration of his return.

They takened me to the Waldorf Astoria, where they had a whole suite of rooms for me. There were two beds in my room. Twin beds. That kinder tickled me. I didn't know which one to sleep in. So I tried them both.

The Tennessee Society done give me a banquet and there were a whole heap of people sitting down to the big dinner. There were generals and statesmen all over the place. They asked me that many questions that I kinder got tired inside of my head and wanted to get up and light out and do some hiking. There were a heap of speeches. They seemed to be having a sorter competition saying nice things about me. They told me I was famous. And I thought to myself, if this is fame, having to stay at a big hotel with several rooms all to yourself and two beds to sleep in and a big banquet where there are so many people you couldn't remember them nohow, then fame ain't the sorter thing I used to think it was.

Of course, everybody was nice. But I'm a-telling you it was a tough corner for a mountain boy to be in. Between answering questions and kinder watching the people around me eat so I would know how to handle that old silverware without making too many bad breaks, I'm a-telling you I was busied a-plenty. But I got through it all right. I didn't know what all the plates and knives and forks and spoons were for. So I kinder slowed up and jes kept a couple of moves behind the others. So I knowed what to do. In the middle of that-there old banquet I got to kinder dreaming about home and the little log cabin and my mother and Gracie and them-there hound dogs of mine. I knowed I was to be with them soon, and I sorter couldn't think of anything else.

Jes the same, everybody was nice and meant well and they all done their best to give me a right-smart time.

Next day I hiked a-plenty all over that old city. So

you see I was still hiking. I done more of that when I was in the Army than anything else.

I tried to get my mother over the long-distance telephone

but we couldn't get through That made me homesicker than ever.

They told me I could have anything I wanted in New York City. I got to figuring it out and I couldn't figure that I wanted anything special. Hit's kinder funny that when you can have anything You want, you don't seem to want anything. That's life. So hit seems to me hit ain't having things that matters so much; hits the wanting to have them that counts. They kept insisting. So I thought I would like to have a ride in the subway. You see I thought it was right smart to have them tunnels under the ground and be able to go all over New York City that way, so they done got a special train and rode me all over New York City in the subway. I liked that, Ho, Ho.

I was looking at New York City. On the night of the 23rd I took the train for Washington, D.C. honorable Hull had come to get me.

May 25, 1918
Washington D.C.

So I got to Washington this morning about 6 A.M. So we drove a car all over Washington almost looking at the city and I had the honor to meet Secretary Baker of war and shake hands with him.

Congressman Cordell Hull takened me in charge and showed me all over Washington, D. C. He takened me to the White House to meet the President, but the President was done gone. So I met Secretary of War Baker. And we talked about the war. And he was most kind and considerate. I went to Congress. They takened me there on the floor of the House. And the members all come around me. And there was more questioning and a whole heap of cheers and applause. By this time I was sorter feeling like a red fox circling when the hounds are after it. I was beginning to wonder if I ever would get back to my own home again.

The next day I went back to New York City again; and they

takened me to the stock exchange in Wall Street. That didn't mean nothing to me nohow. A country boy like me jes couldn't understand what it was all about. Rifle-guns, hounds, foxes, coons, mountains, shootin' matches-I understand these things. I belong to them and I'm a-thinking they belong to me. But money and big business were things I jes didn't understand nohow. The streets in that part of New York City are most awful narrow and plumb full of people. I figured it was sorter funny that people would be willing to crowd together and work and live in such cramped-up spaces when there's such a heap of open country and grass and sky in other parts of America. But then you see I was a country boy and didn't understand the city life.

About this time they begun to pester me with a whole heap of offers to go on the stage and into the movies. They offered so much money that it almost takened my breath away. I thought to myself, wouldn't I look funny in tights, ho, ho. Besides, I sorter felt that to take money like that would be commercializing my uniform and my soldiering. I knowed if I hadn't been to war and hadn't been a doughboy they never would have offered me nothing nohow. I also knowed I didn't go to war to make a whole heap of money, or to go on the stage or in the movies. I went over there to help make peace. And there was peace now. So I didn't take their thirty pieces of silver and betray that-there old uniform of mine. I would have been interested in helping to make the pictures if I didn't have to be in it myself and if they would do it, not to make a heap of money for themselves or for me but jes to show what the boys done done over there, and also to show what faith will do for you if you believe in it right. But I knowed they weren't interested in that. They jes wanted me to show how I done killed the Germans in the Argonne. So I wouldn't have nothing to do with them nohow. They also offered me a heap of money to write newspaper stories and to sign advertisements. But I didn't want to do that either.

I jes wanted to be left alone to go back to my beginnings. The war was over. I had done done my job and I had done it the bestest I could. So I figured I ought to be left alone and allowed to go home to the mountains where I belonged. I sorter felt, too, that if they wanted to do something right smart for me they might help me to get a soon-go for home. The Army officers understood me and I understood them and they sent me South to be demobilized as soon as they could get the papers fixed up.

I'm a-saying right here that they treated me right smart all the time that I was in the Army. They done played the game with me and they played square. So far as I am concerned the officers and everybody connected with the Army done done the right thing by me. They were right-smart folk.

In late May I got my transportation papers to Ft. Oglethorpe, Ga., and there I got my discharge papers and transportation home. But I can't tell you what I felt like when I got home in May, 1919. The mountains sure looked good to me. The mountain people, thousands of them, come from all over jes to say howdy. All of my big brothers were there and my sisters and my mother.

As soon as I got back to the little old log cabin in the Valley of the Three Forks of the Wolf I went a-hunting-not—for coon, or possum or fox or squirrels—I went a-hunting for Gracie. I done found her too. And what I said to her and what she said to me and what we said to each other ain't nobody's business nohow.

Then I went out on the mountainside where I used to pray and when it was all quiet and there was nobody around nohow, I returned thanks to God. He had given me my assurance that even if I didn't think it right I should go jes the same; and would be protected from harm; and would come back without a hair of my head injured. I don't know what I said to Him. I disremember. I don't know that I said anything. I jes felt.

And, oh, my, what a joyful time I had with them-there hound dogs of mine. I done set down and looked at them and patted them and they wagged their tails and licked my hands, and then, Ho, Ho, they bayed and sorter circled round, and sorter lit out for the woods; jes to sorter remind me that they hadn't been foolin' round nohow while I was away, and they still knowed where the coons and possums and the foxes were.

In a few days I had the old uniform off and the overalls on. I done cleaned up the old muzzle-loader. It was all over. I was home.

York actually preferred to live in the wilds of Tennessee than in the fancy city of New York and Washington. Give him a rifle and a couple of hunting dogs and he was a happy man. Fame never really meant much to him.

CHAPTER 30

HEAP O' LARNIN'

Nothing seemed to have changed much. The little old log cabin was still there at the head of the spring and the water in it was a-running and a-singing the same as ever. The razorbacks were rooting for acorns and hickory nuts jes as before. Their bells, and the cow bells, too, sounded much the same. The dogwood blossomed white and the red-bud pinkish-like, jes as they used to. Though I seemed to notice them more now. The hills were as they always were, blue and kinder dreamy. And the people hadn't changed nohow. They were putting in their crops, working from sunup to sundown.

The same crowd of mountain boys and girls were to be seen at the store. The little church on the hill was doing tol'able well. Rosier Pile held his Sunday school the same and the kiddies larned their lessons and some of them fell off to sleep jes about the same.

The war had come and gone. Millions of boys had been killed and wounded. Millions of dollars had been poured out jes like water. Homes all over the world had been desolated. Some of the old countries had been all mussed up and new ones had come up and sort of takened their places. The whole outside world seemed to have changed. But not our valley. Everything there was kinder the same.

But I knowed, though, that I had done changed. I knowed I wasn't like I used to be. The big outside world I had been in and the things I had fought through had teched me up inside a most powerful lot. The old life I had lived seemed a long, long way behind me. It seemed to be a sort of other life in another world. I knowed I had changed. I was sort of restless and full of dreams and wanting to be doing something; and I didn't understand. So I sat out on the hillside trying to puzzle it out.

Before the war I had never been out of the mountains. I had never wanted to be. I had sorter figured that them-there mountains were our shield against the iniquities of the outside world. They sorter isolated us and kept us together so that we might grow up pureblooded and resourceful and God-loving and God-fearing people. They done done that, too, but they done more'n that. They done kept out many of the good and worthwhile things like good roads, schools, libraries, up-to-date homes, and modern farming methods. But I never thought of these things before going to war. Only when I got back home again and got to kinder thinking and dreaming, I sorter realized hit.

Then I knowed we had to have them. We jes had to. And the more I thought the more I kinder figured that all of my trials and tribulations in the war had been to prepare me for doing just this work in the mountains. All of my suffering in having to go and kill were to teach me to value human lives. All the temptations I done went through were to strengthen my character. All the associations with my buddies were to help me understand and love my brother man. All of the pains I done seed and went through were to help and prepare me. And the fame and fortunes they done offered me in the cities were to try me out and see if I was fitted for the work He, wanted me to do.

Again the Devil taketh him into an exceedingly high mountain and showeth him all the kingdoms of the world, and the glory of them; and he said unto him, all these things will I give thee, if thou wilt fall down and worship me. Then saith Jesus unto him, get thee hence, Satan, for it is written, thou shalt worship the Lord thy God and Him only shalt thou serve.

So He was tempted. So everybody since, who is called on to do good, is tempted. So I, an unlarned mountain boy, was tempted too.

But I done come through it all all right. My prayers and the prayers of my mother and Pastor Pile and a whole heap of other friends were answered.

So I talked to Gracie about these dreams of mine. She understood. She done always understood. So we done got married. Governor Roberts, the Governor of Tennessee, done come down to our valley and performed the ceremony. Thousands of people come from all over Tennessee to see the goings-on. And the mountain people provided the vittles. They brought in goats and hogs and turkeys and slaughtered and dressed them right there on the hillside. They set up a table, the largest I ever seed, and they done piled hit up with all the meats and eggs there was and with sweet potatoes and cornbread and milk and jams and cakes and a whole mess of other things. We were married on the mountainside above the spring and under the shady trees and with the blue mountains and green grass and the flowers all around.

Then I begun what I felt was my life work. I went to the State Highway Department and asked them to build a road through the mountains. And they done done it. They built what we now call the York Highway right across our county. Then the other counties done noticed it and built roads on either end. And to-day we have a right-smart road running through this-here mountain country. And there were only mountain trails and old dirt roads that were no good nohow and creek beds here before. That was the beginning.

Then I begun to work for a school, an up-to-date school in our county. We done needed it most awful bad. We only had a few schools here. They were all frame buildings, and some of them were well-nigh uninhabitable. There was only one high school. Very few of the teachers were college graduates. So, you see, we needed new buildings and up-to-date teachers and equipment most awful bad. So I raised about $15,000 myself and the state and the county each put up $50,000. That gave me $115,000 to build new schools. I wanted a modern, up-to-date vocational school, which later on could be sorter developed into a mountain college. The Board they give me couldn't see things the way I did. So I have had a most awful hard fight, a much worser one than the one I had with the machine guns in the Argonne.

The politicians and the real estate People tried to use me. The small-town bankers tried to get in on it. Jealous factions wanted to get a-hold of it and handle it their way. So it done got held up. And oh, my, I had a terrible time. But I knowed I was in the right. So I kept on fighting jes the same. I done got the old Board put out. I done got the State Board of Education to handle the promotion. The school is a quasistate institution to-day. And hit's a-coming. At this moment we have two fine new school buildings with right-smart teachers and up-to-date equipment in Jimtown. And that's only the beginnings.

As soon as I can get the money to make them self-supporting, and have proven that I can successfully look after them I'm a-thinking they're a-going to be handed over to me. And then I'm a-planning to sorter turn them into a mountain college for vocational education. I'm a-going to teach the mountain boys and girls the trades; dairying, wood-working, carpentering, fruit growing, the breeding of pure-bred livestock, dressmaking, and so on. I'm going to have them instructed in health and hygiene. I'm going to train them to be self-supporting.

If they're too poor to pay their way I'm a-going to give them a chance to work their way through. If they live back in the mountains where the roads are too bad to get out I'm a-going to build good roads to them. I don't know of no part of America nohow that needs all of this worser than we do. In our county alone there are over one thousand boys and girls between the ages of six and eighteen that can't even read and write. And I'm a-felling you it's not their fault.

Some of the boys and girls who are going to our two schools to-day walk two miles through the mountains out to the highway, where they catch the school buses and then ride fourteen miles to school; then after the school is over they have to return the same way. I kinder think that boys and girls who will do this day after day, week after week, right through the school year, want and deserve a chance to git larnin' most awful bad.

Whenever I go away on a trip for the schools they meet me as soon as I git back and ask me haven't I got more money, so that they can get more larning'. I'm a-telling you hit kinder gives me my assurance again that I am right, dreaming and planning these things for them. That ain't all nohow. I'm a-planning playgrounds for the children, too, and libraries and a medical and nursing system.

Of course, in such things as electric lighting, sewage, water supply, and up-to-date homes our mountain towns and villages are sorter away behind the times. But I'm a-thinking if I can bring larnin' to the children they will grow up and change all these things. I can't influence the older people much nohow. They're sorter set in their ways. But if I can get the children to school and to college, the rest will come.

I ain't had much larnin' myself; so I know what an awful handicap that is. I'm a-trying all the time now to overcome that and improve myself. I ain't had much business experience neither, but I'm working hard to get that. I don't know much about finance, but I know I am honest and I am larnin' to handle money tol'ably.

I am blessed with a whole heap of most loyal and powerful friends all over America; and I still have and always will have my faith in God. I know He will not fail to help me. So I'm getting along tol'able well. Hit's a-coming-that dream of mine. I'm a-going some day to have roads all through these here mountains; to have modern homes and all sorts of other improvements and sanitary arrangements in our towns and villages; and most of all, to have a heap of schools and a right-smart mountain college.

I ain't going to show any favouritism nohow. I fought with Catholics and Protestants, with Jews, Greeks, Italians, Poles, and Irish, as well as American borned boys in the World War. They were buddies of mine and I larned to love them. If there is any of them in these-here mountains we'll make a place for them in these schools. I'm a-going to give all the children in the mountains the chance that's a-coming to them. I'm a-going to bring them a heap o' larnin'.

The End

Editor's note:

For further study on the life of Alvin York refer to an excellent book called, *Sgt. York His Life, Legend & Legacy* authored by John Perry, published by, Broadman & Holman available at most book dealers.

Tour the Alvin C. York Home in Pall Mall, TN
2700 North York Hwy., Pall Mall, TN 38577
Phone 931-879-6465

Visit the Memorial War Building in Nashville, Tennessee where his uniform, medals and sundry items are displayed. Nashville Chamber of Commerce 615-259-4755

© by Underwood & Underwood

ON THE S. S. *OHIOAN*

Sergeant York as he returned from France after accomplishing what was said to be the greatest individual feat of the war.

"From his father he inherited physical courage, from his mother moral courage—and both spent their lives developing those qualities of manhood in their boy."

SERGEANT ALVIN C. YORK

"Marshal Foch, in decorating him, said· 'What you did was the greatest thing accomplished by any private soldier of all of the armies of Europe.'"

"Back again at his home in the 'Valley of the Three Forks o' the Wolf' he asked that the people give him no more gifts, but instead contribute the money to a fund to build simple, primary schools for the children of the mountains who had no schools. Of the fund, not a dollar was to be for his personal use, nor for any effort he might put forth in its behalf."

"Before Sergeant York went to war he had given an option to his mountain sweetheart—she could have him for the takin' when he got back."

Sergeant York, his bride and his mother, the guests of Governor Roberts of Tennessee and Mrs. Roberts at the Governor's Mansion.

PREACHING ON THE MOUNTAINSIDE

"I hed been living for God and working in the church work sometime before I joined the army."

YORK AGRICULTURAL COLLEGE

(The Grade School)

"I'm goin' to give all the mountain children a chance to get a heap o' larnin'."

SERGT. YORK AT THE TOMB OF PRESIDENT JACKSON

"The bone and sinew of the army of General Jackson, in his Indian campaigns and against the British at New Orleans, were the riflemen of Tennessee and Kentucky."

HUNTING COMPANIONS

"I jes couldn't hope to be happy nohow if I couldn't hunt and shoot and tramp around these-here hills with them-there hound-dogs of mine."

SPOILS FOR THE VICTOR

"I jes knowed I was a-goin' to have a turkey dinner that night, ho ho."

IN A PEACE-TIME SETTING

Sergeant Alvin C. York and his three sons in front of their home in the Valley of the Three Forks of the Wolf.

LLOYD GEORGE
SIR DOUGLAS HAIG
WOODROW WILSON
GENERAL PERSHING
MARSHAL FOCH
Giants of Democracy

CHRONOLOGY OF WORLD WAR

Comprehensive Chronology of the Four Years of War—Dates of Important Battles and Naval Engagements—Ready Reference of Historical Events from June, 1914, to End of War in 1918.

1914

June 28—Archduke Ferdinand and wife assassinated in Sarajevo, Bosnia.

July 28—Austria-Hungary declares war on Serbia.

August 1—Germany declares war on Russia and general mobilization is under way in France and Austria-Hungary. **Aug. 2**—German troops enter France at Cirey; Russian troops enter Germany at Schwidden; German army enters Luxemburg over protest, and Germany asks Belgium for free passage of her troops. **Aug. 3**—British fleet mobilizes; Belgium appeals to Great Britain for diplomatic aid and German ambassador quits Paris.

Aug. 4—France declares war on Germany; Germany declares war on Belgium; Great Britain sends Belgium neutrality ultimatum to Germany; British army mobilized and state of war between Great Britain and Germany is declared. President Wilson issues neutrality proclamation. **Aug. 5**—Germans begin fighting on Belgium frontier; Germany asks for Italy's help. **Aug. 6**—Austria declares war on Russia. **Aug. 7**—Germans defeated by French at Altkirch. **Aug. 9**—Germans capture Liege. Portugal announces it will support Great Britain; British land troops in France. **Aug. 10**—France declares war on Austria-Hungary.

Aug. 12—Great Britain declares war on Austria-Hungary; Montenegro declares war on Germany. **Aug. 15**—Japan sends ultimatum to Germany to withdraw from Japanese and Chinese waters and evacuate Kiao-chow; Russia offers autonomy to Poland. **Aug. 20**—German army enters Brussels. **Aug. 23**—Japan declares war on Germany; Russia victorious in battles in East Prussia. **Aug. 24**—Japanese warships bombard Tsingtao. **Aug. 25**—Japan and Austria break off diplomatic relations. **Aug. 28**—English win naval battle over German fleet near Helgoland. **Aug. 29**—Germans defeat Russians at Allenstein; occupy Amiens; advance to La Fere, sixty-five miles from Paris.

September 1—Germans cross Marne; bombs dropped on Paris; Turkish army mobilized; Zeppelins drop bombs on Antwerp. **Sept. 2**—Government of France transferred to Bordeaux; Russians capture Lemberg. **Sept. 4**—Germans cross the Marne. **Sept. 5**—England, France, and Russia sign pact to make no separate peace. **Sept. 6**—French win battle of Marne; British cruiser Path finder sunk in North sea by a German submarine. **Sept. 7**—Germans retreat from the Marne. **Sept. 14**—Battle of Aisne starts; German retreat halted. **Sept. 15**—First battle of Soissons fought. **Sept. 20**—Russians capture Jaroslau and begin siege of Przemysl.

October 9-10—Germans capture Antwerp. **Oct. 12**—Germans take Ghent. **Oct. 20**—Fighting along Yser river begins. **Oct. 29**—Turkey begins war on Russia.

November 7—Tsingtro falls before Japanese troops. **Nov. 9**—German cruiser Emden destroyed.

December 11—German advance on Warsaw checked. **Dec. 14**—Belgrade recaptured by Serbians. **Dec. 16**—German cruisers bombard Scarborough, Hartlepool, and Whitby, on English coast, killing fifty or more persons; Austrians said to have lost upwards of 100,000 men in Serbian defeat. **Dec. 25**—Italy occupies Avlona, Albania.

CHRONOLOGY OF THE WORLD WAR

1915

January 1—British battleship Formidable sunk. **Jan.** 8—Roumania mobilizes 750,000 men; violent fighting in the Argonne. **Jan.** 11—Germans cross the Rawka, thirty miles from Warsaw. **Jan.** 24—British win naval battle in North sea. **Jan.** 29—Russian army invades Hungary; German efforts to cross Aisne repulsed.

February 1—British repel strong German attack near La Bassee. **Feb.** 2—Turks are defeated in attack on Suez canal. **Feb.** 4— Russians capture Tarnow in Galicia. **Feb.** 8—Turks along Suez canal in full retreat; Turkish land defenses at the Dardanelles shelled by British torpedo boats. **Feb.** 11—Germans evacuate Lodz. **Feb.** 12—Germans drive Russians from positions in East Prussia, taking 26,000 prisoners. **Feb.** 14—Russians report capture of fortifications at Smolnik. **Feb.** 16—Germans capture Plock and Bielsk in Poland; French capture two miles of German trenches in Champagne district.

February 17—Germans report they have taken 50,000 Russian prisoners in Mazurian lake district. **Feb.** 18—German blockade of English and French coasts put into effect. **Feb.** 19-20—British and French fleets bombard Dardanelles forts. **Feb.** 21—American steamer Evelyn sunk by mine in North sea. **Feb.** 22—German war office announces capture of 100,000 Russian prisoners in engagements in Mazurian lake region; American steamer Carib sunk by mine in North sea. **Feb.** 28—Dardanelles entrance forts capitulate to English and French.

March 4—Landing of allied troops on both sides of Dardanelles straits reported; German U-4 sunk by French destroyers. **March** 10—Battle of Neuve Chapelle begins. **March** 14—German cruiser Dresden sunk in Pacific by English. **March** 18—British battleships Irresistible and Ocean and French battleship Bouvet sunk in Dardanelles strait. **March** 22—Fort of Przemysl surrenders to Russians. **March** 23—Allies land troops on Gallipoli peninsula. **March** 25—Russians victorious over Austrians in Carpathians.

April 8—German auxiliary cruiser, Prinz Eitel Friedrich, interned at Newport News, Va. **April** 16—Italy has 1,200,000 men mobilized under arms; Austrians report complete defeat of Russians in Carpathian campaign. **April** 23—Germans force way across Ypres canal and take 1,600 prisoners. **April** 25—Allies stop German drive on Ypres line in Belgium. **April** 29—British report regaining of two-thirds of lost ground in Ypres battle.

May 7—Liner Lusitania torpedoed and sunk by German submarine off the coast of Ireland with the loss of more than 1,000 lives, 102 Americans. **May** 9—French advance two and one-half miles against German forces north of Arras, taking 2,000 prisoners. **May** 23—Italy declares war on Austria.

June 3—Germans recapture Przemysl with Austrian help. **June** 18—British suffer defeat north of La Bassee canal. **June** 28—Italians enter Austrian territory south of Riva on western shore of Lake Garda.

July 3—Tolmino falls into Italian hands. **July** 9—British make gains north of Ypres and French retake trenches in the Vosges. **July** 13—Germans defeated in the Argonne. **July** 29—Warsaw evacuated; Lublin captured by Austrians.

August 4—Germans occupy Warsaw. **Aug.** 14—Austrians and Germans concentrate 400,000 soldiers on Serbian frontier. **Aug.** 21—Italy declares war on Turkey.

September 1—Ambassador Bernstorff announces Germans will sink no more liners without warning. **Sept.** 4—German submarine torpedoes liner Hesperian. **Sept.** 9—Germans make air raid on London, killing twenty persons and wounding 100 others; United States asks Austria to recall **Ambassador**

Dumba. **Sept.** 20—Germans begin drive on Serbia to open route to Turkey. **Sept.** 22—Russian army retreating from Vilna, escapes German encircling movement. **Sept.** 25-30—Battle of Champagne, resulting in great advance for allied armies and causing Kaiser Wilhelm to rush to the west front; German counter attacks repulsed.

October 5—Russia and Bulgaria sever diplomatic relations; Russian, French, British, Italian, and Serbian diplomatic representatives ask for passports in Sofia. **Oct.** 10—Gen. Mackensen's forces take Belgrade. **Oct.** 12—Edith Cavell executed by Germans. **Oct.** 13—Bulgaria declares war on Serbia. **Oct.** 15—Great Britain declares war on Bulgaria. **Oct.** 16—France declares war on Bulgaria. **Oct.** 19—Russia and Italy declare war on Bulgaria. **Oct.** 27—Germans join Bulgarians in northeastern Serbia and open way to Constantinople. **Oct.** 30—Germans defeated at Mitau.

November 9—Italian liner Ancona torpedoed.

December 1—British retreat from near Bagdad. **Dec.** 4—Ford "peace party" sails for Europe. **Dec.** 8-9—Allies defeated in Macedonia. **Dec.** 15—Sir John Douglas Haig succeeds Sir John French as chief of English armies on west front.

1916

January 8—British troops at Kut-el-Amara surrounded. **Jan.** 9—British evacuate Gallipoli peninsula. **Jan.** 13—Austrians capture Cetinje, capital of Montenegro. **Jan.** 23—Scutari, capital of Albania, captured by Austrians.

February 22—Crown prince's army begins attack on Verdun.

March 8—Germany declares war on Portugal. **March** 15—Austria-Hungary declares war on Portugal. **March** 24—Steamer Sussex torpedoed and sunk.

April 18—President Wilson sends note to Germany. **April** 19—President Wilson speaks to congress, explaining diplomatic situation. **April** 24—Insurrection in Dublin. **April** 29—British troops at Kut-el-Amara surrender to Turks. **April** 30—Irish revolution suppressed.

May 3—Irish leaders of insurrection executed. **May** 4—Germany makes promise to change methods of submarine warfare. **May** 13—Austrians begin great offensive against Italians in Trentino. **May** 31—Great naval battle off Danish coast.

June 5—Lord Kitchener lost with cruiser Hampshire. **June** 11—Russians capture Dubno. **June** 29—Sir Roger Casement sentenced to be hanged for treason

July 1—British and French begin great offensive on the Somme. **July** 6—David Lloyd George appointed secretary of war. **July** 9—German merchant submarine Deutschland arrives at Baltimore. **July** 23—Gen. Kuropatkin's army wins battle near Riga. **July** 27—English take Delville wood; Serbian forces begin attack on Bulgars in Macedonia.

August 2—French take Fleury. **Aug.** 3—Sir Roger Casement executed for treason. **Aug.** 4—French recapture Thiaumont for fourth time; British repulse Turkish attack on Suez canal. **Aug.** 7—Italians on Isonzo front capture Monte Sabotino and Monte San Michele. **Aug.** 8—Turks force Russian evacuation of Bitlis and Mush. **Aug.** 9—Italians cross Isonzo river and occupy Austrian city of Goeritz. **Aug.** 10—Austrians evacuate Stanislau; allies take Doiran, near Saloniki, from Bulgarians.

August 19—German submarines sink British light cruisers Nottingham and Falmouth. **Aug.** 24—French occupy Maurepas, north of the Somme; Russians recapture Mush in Armenia. **Aug.** 27—Italy declares war on Germany; Roumania enters war on side of allies. **Aug.** 29—Field Marshal von Hindenburg made chief of staff of German armies, succeeding Gen. von Falkenhayn. **August** 30—Russian armies seize all five passes in Carpathians into Hungary.

September 3—Allies renew offensive north of Somme; Bulgarian and German troops invade Dobrudja, in Roumania. **Sept.** 7—Germans and Bulgarians capture Roumanian fortress of Tutrakan; Roumanians take Orsova, Bulgarian city. **Sept.** 19—German-Bulgarian army captures Roumanian fortress of Silistria. **Sept.** 14—British for first time use "tanks." **Sept.** 15—Italians begin new offensive on Carso.

October 2—Roumanian army of invasion in Bulgaria defeated by Germans and Bulgarians under Von Mackensen. **Oct.** 4—German submarines sink French cruiser Gallia and Cunard liner Franconia. **Oct.** 8—German submarines sink six merchant steamships off Nantucket, Mass. **Oct.** 11—Greek seacoast forts dismantled and turned over to allies on demand of England and France. **Oct.** 23—German-Bulgar armies capture Constanza, Roumania **Oct.** 24—French win back Douaumont, Thiaumont field work, Haudromont quarries, and Caillette wood near Verdun, in smash of two miles.

November 1—Italians, in new offensive on the Carso plateau, capture 5,000 Austrians. **Nov.** 2—Germans evacuate Fort Vaux at Verdun. **Nov.** 5—Germans and Austrians proclaim new kingdom of Poland, of territory captured from Russia. **Nov.** 6—Submarine sinks British passenger steamer Arabia. **Nov.** 7—Cardinal Mercier protests against German deportation of Belgians; submarine sinks American steamer Columbian. **Nov.** 8—Russian army invades Transylvania, Hungary. **Nov.** 9—Austro-German armies defeat Russians in Volhyina and take 4,000 prisoners.

November 13—British launch new offensive in Somme region on both sides of Ancre. **Nov.** 14—British capture fortified village of Beacourt, near the Ancre. **Nov.** 19—Serbian, French, and Russian troops recapture Monastir; Germans cross Transylvania Alps and enter western Roumania. **Nov.** 21—British hospital ship Britannic sunk by mine in Aegean sea. **Nov.** 23—Roumanian army retreats ninety miles from Bucharest. **Nov.** 24—German-Bulgarian armies take Orsova and Turnu-Severin from Roumanians. **Nov.** 25—Greek provisional government declares war on Germany and Bulgaria. **Nov.** 28—Roumanian government abandons Bucharest and moves capital to Jassy.

December 5—Premier Herbert Asquith of England resigns. **Dec.** 7—David Lloyd George accepts British premiership. **Dec.** 8—Gen. von Mackensen captures big Roumanian army in Prohova valley. **Dec.** 12—Chancellor von Bethman-Hollweg announces in reichstag that Germany will propose peace; new cabinet in France under Aristide Briand as premier, and Gen. Robert Georges Nivelle given chief of command of French army. **Dec.** 15—French at Verdun win two miles of front and capture 11,000.

December 19—Llloyd George declines German peace proposals. **Dec.** 23—Baron Burian succeeded as minister of foreign affairs in Austria by Count Czernin. **Dec.** 26—Germany proposes to President Wilson "an immediate meeting of delegates of the belligerents." **Dec** 27—Russians defeated in five-day battle in eastern Wallachia, Roumania.

1917

January 1—Submarine sinks British transport Ivernia. **Jan.** 9—Russian premier, Trepoff, resigns. Golitzin succeeds him. **Jan.** 31—Germany announces unrestricted submarine warfare.

February 3—President Wilson reviews submarine controversy before congress; United States severs diplomatic relations with Germany; American steamer Housatonic sunk without warning. **Feb.** 7—Senate indorses President's act of breaking off diplomatic relations. **Feb. 12**—United States refuses German request to discuss matters of difference unless Germany withdraws unrestricted submarine warfare order.

February 14—Von Bernstorff sails for Germany. **Feb. 25**—British under Gen. Maude capture Kut-el-Amara; submarine sinks liner Laconia without warning; many lost including two Americans. **Feb. 26**—President Wilson asks congress for authority to arm American merchantships. **Feb. 28**—Secretary Lansing makes public Zimmerman note to Mexico, proposing Mexican-Japanese-German alliance.

March 9—President Wilson calls extra session of congress for April 16. **March 11**—British under Gen. Maude capture Bagdad; revolution starts in Petrograd. **March 15**—Czar Nicholas of Russia abdicates. **March 17**—French and British capture Bapaume. **March 18**—New French ministry formed by Alexander Ribot.

March 21—Russian forces cross Persian border into Turkish territory; American oil steamer Healdton torpedoed without warning. **March 22**—United States recognizes new government of Russia. **March 27**—Gen. Murray's British expedition into the Holy Land defeats Turkish army near Gaza.

April 2—President Wilson asks congress to declare that acts of Germany constitute a state of war; submarine sinks American steamer Aztec without warning. **April 4**—United States senate passes resolution declaring a state of war exists with Germany. **April 6**—House passes war resolution and President Wilson signs joint resolution of congress. **April 8**—Austria declares severance of diplomatic relations with United States.

April 9—British defeat Germans at Vimy Ridge and take 6,000 prisoners; United States seizes fourteen Austrian interned ships. **April 20**—Turkey severs diplomatic relations with the U. S. **April 28**—Congress passes selective service act for raising of army of 500,000; Guatemala severs diplomatic relations with Germany.

May 7—War department orders raising of nine volunteer regiments of engineers to go to France. **May 14**—Espionage act becomes law by passing senate. **May 18**—President Wilson signs selective service act. Also directs expeditionary force of regulars under Gen. Pershing to go to France. **May 19**—Congress passes war appropriation bill of $3,000,000,000.

June 5—Nearly 10,000,000 men in U. S. register for military service. **June 12**—King Constantine of Greece abdicates. **June 13**—Gen. Pershing and staff arrive in Paris. **June 15**—First Liberty loan closes with large oversubscription. **June 26**—First contingent American troops under Gen. Sibert arrives in France. **June 29**—Greece severs diplomatic relations with Teutonic allies.

July 9—President Wilson drafts state militia into federal service. Also places food and fuel under federal control. **July 13**—War department order drafts 678,000 men into military service. **July 14**—Aircraft appropriation bill of $640,000,000 passes house; Chancellor von Bethmann-Hollweg's resignation forced by German political crisis.

July 18—United States government orders censorship of telegrams and cablegrams crossing frontiers. **July 19**—New German Chancellor Michaelis declares Germany will not war for conquest; radicals and Catholic party ask peace without forced acquisitions of territory. **July 22**—Siam declares war on Germany. **July 23**—Premier Kerensky given unlimited powers in Russia. **July 28**—United States war industries board created to supervise expenditures.

August 25—Italian Second army breaks through Austrian line on Isonzo front. **Aug. 28**—President Wilson rejects Pope Benedict's peace plea.

September 10—Gen. Korniloff demands control of Russian government. **Sept.** 11—Russian deputies vote to support Kerensky. Korniloff's generals ordered arrested. **Sept.** 16—Russia proclaims new republic by order of Premier Kerensky. **Sept.** 20—Gen. Haig advances mile through German lines at Ypres. **Sept.** 21—Gen. Tasker H. Bliss named chief of staff, U. S. army.

October 16—Germans occupy islands of Runo and Adro in the Gulf of Riga. **Oct.** 25—French under Gen. Petain advance and take 12,000 prisoners on Aisne front. **Oct.** 27—Formal announcement made that American troops in France had fired their first shots in the war. **Oct.** 29—Italian Isonzo front collapses and Austro-German army reaches outposts of Udine.

November 1—Secretary Lansing makes public the Luxburg "spurlos versenkt" note. **Nov.** 7—Austro-German troops capture? **Nov.** 9—Permanent interallied military commission created. **Nov.** 24—Navy department announces capture of first German submarine by American destroyer. **Nov.** 28—Bolsheviki get absolute control of Russian assembly in Russian elections.

December 6—Submarine sinks the Jacob Jones, first regular warship of American navy destroyed. **Dec.** 7—Congress declares war on Austria-Hungary. **Dec.** 8—Jerusalem surrenders to Gen. Allenby's forces.

1918

January 5—President Wilson delivers speech to congress giving "fourteen points" necessary to peace. **Jan.** 20—British monitors win seafight with cruisers Goeben and Breslau, sinking latter. **Jan.** 28—Russia and Roumania sever diplomatic relations.

February 2—United States troops take over their first sector, near Toul. **Feb.** 6—United States troopship Tuscania sunk by submarine, 126 lost. **Feb.** 11— President Wilson, in address to congress, gives four additional peace principles, including self-determination of nations; Bolsheviki declare war with Germany over, but refuse to sign peace treaty. **Feb.** 13—Bolo Pasha sentenced to death in France for treason. **Feb.** 25—Germans take Reval, Russian naval base, and Pskov; Chancellor von Hertling agrees "in principle" with President Wilson's peace principles, in address to reichstag.

March 1—Americans repulse German attack on Toul sector. **March** 2—Treaty of peace with Germany signed by Bolsheviki at Brest-Litovsk. **March** 4—Germany and Roumania sign armistice on German terms. **March** 13—German troops occupy Odessa. **March** 14—All Russian congress of soviets ratifies peace treaty. **March** 21—German spring offensive starts on fifty mile front. **March** 22—Germans take 16,000 British prisoners and 200 guns.

March 23—German drive gains nine miles. "Mystery gun" shells Paris. **March** 24—Germans reach the Somme, gaining fifteen miles. American engineers rushed to aid British. **March** 25—Germans take Bapaume. **March** 27—Germans take Albert. **March** 28—British counter attack and gain; French take three towns; Germans advance toward Amiens. **March** 29—"Mystery gun" kills seventy-five churchgoers in Paris on Good Friday.

April 4—Germans start second phase of their spring drive on the Somme. **April** 10—Germans take 10,000 British prisoners in Flanders. **April** 16—Germans capture Messines ridge, near Ypres; Bolo Pasha executed. **April** 23—British and French navies "bottle up" Zeebrugge. **April** 26—Germans capture Mount Kemmel, taking 6,500 prisoners.

May 5—Austria starts drive on Italy. **May** 10—British navy bottles up Ostend. **May** 24—British ship Moldavia, carrying American troops, torpedoed; 56 lost. **May** 27—Germans begin third phase of drive on west front; gain five miles. **May** 28—Germans take 15,000 prisoners in drive. **May** 29—Germans take Soissons and menace Reims. American troops capture Cantigny. **May**

30—Germans reach the Marne, fifty-five miles from Paris. **May 31**—Germans take 45,000 prisoners in drive.

June 1—Germans advance nine miles; are forty-six miles from Paris. **June 3**—Five German submarines attack U. S. coast and sink eleven ships. **June 5**—U. S. marines fight on the Marne near Chateau Thierry. **June 9**—Germans start fourth phase of their drive by advancing toward Noyon. **June 10**—Germans gain two miles. U. S. marines capture south end of Belleau wood.

June 12—French and Americans start counter attack. **June 15**—Austrians begin another drive on Italy and take 16,000 prisoners. **June 17**—Italians check Austrians on Piave river. **June 19**—Austrians cross the Piave. **June 22**—Italians defeat Austrians on the Piave. **June 23**—Austrians begin great retreat across the Piave.

July 18—Gen. Foch launches allied offensive, with French, American, British, Italian and Belgian troops. **July 21**—Americans and French capture Chateau Thierry. **July 30**—German crown prince flees from the Marne and withdraws army.

August 2—Soissons recaptured by Foch. **Aug. 4**—Americans take Fismes. **Aug. 5**—American troops landed at Archangel. **Aug. 7**—Americans cross the Vesle. **Aug. 16**—Bapaume recaptured. **Aug. 28**—French recross the Somme.

September 1—Foch retakes Peronne. **Sept. 12**—Americans launch successful attack in St. Mihiel salient. **Sept. 28**—Allies win on 250 mile line, from North sea to Verdun. **Sept. 29**—Allies cross Hindenburg line. **Sept. 30**—Bulgaria surrenders, after successful allied campaign in Balkans. **October 1**—French take St. Quentin. **Oct. 4**—Austria asks Holland to mediate with allies for peace. **Oct. 5**—Germans start abandonment of Lille and burn Douai. **Oct. 6**—Germany asks President Wilson for armistice. **Oct. 7**—Americans capture hills around Argonne. **Oct. 8**—President Wilson refuses armistice. **Oct. 9**—Allies capture Cambrai. **Oct. 10**—Allies capture Le Cateau. **Oct. 11**—American transport Otranto torpedoed and sunk; 500 lost. **Oct. 13**—Foch's troops take Laon and La Fere.

October 14—British and Belgians take Roulers; President Wilson demands surrender by Germany. **Oct. 15**—British and Belgians cross Lys river, take 12,000 prisoners and 100 guns. **Oct. 16**—Allies enter Lille outskirts. **Oct. 17**—Allies capture Lille, Bruges, Zeebrugge, Ostend, and Douai. **Oct. 18**—Czecho-Slovaks issue declaration of independence; Czechs rebel and seize Prague, captial of Bohemia; French take Thielt.

October 19—President Wilson refuses Austrian peace plea and says Czecho-Slovak state must be considered. **Oct. 21**—Allies cross the Oise and threaten Valenciennes. **Oct. 22**—Haig's forces cross the Scheldt. **Oct. 23**—President Wilson refuses latest German peace plea. **Oct. 27**—German government asks President Wilson to state terms. **Oct. 28**—Austria begs for separate peace.

October 29—Austria opens direct negotiations with Secretary Lansing. **Oct. 30**—Italians inflict great defeat on Austria; capture 33,000 Austrians evacuating Italian territory. **Oct. 31**—Turkey surrenders; Austrians utterly routed by Italians; lose 50,000; Austrian envoys, under white flag, enter Italian lines.

November 1—Italians pursue beaten Austrians across Tagliamento river; allied conference at Versailles fixes peace terms for Germany. **Nov. 3**—Austria signs armistice amounting virtually to unconditional surrender. **Nov. 4**—Allied terms are sent to Germany. **Nov. 7**—Germany's envoys enter allied lines by arrangement.

November 9—Kaiser Wilhelm abdicates and crown prince renounces throne. **Nov. 10**—Former Kaiser Wilhelm and his eldest son, Friedrick Wilhelm, flee to Holland to escape widespread revolution throughout Germany.

CHRONOLOGY OF THE WORLD WAR

November 9—Kaiser Wilhelm abdicates and crown prince renounces throne. British battleship Britannia torpedoed and sunk by German submarine off entrance to Straits of Gibraltar. **Nov. 10**—Formeer Kaiser Wilhelm and his eldest son, Frederick Wilhelm, flee to Holland to escape widespread revolution throughout Germany. King of Bavaria abdicates. **Nov. 11**—Armistice signed at 11 o'clock a. m., Paris time. Firing ceased on all fronts. An American battery from Providence, Rhode Island, fired last shot at exactly 11 o'clock on the front northwest of Verdun. Germans began evacuation of Belgium and Alsace-Lorraine.

November 12—German republic proclaimed at Berlin. Emperor Charles of Austria abdicates. Belgium demands complete independence instead of guaranteed neutrality. To secure status as a belligerent at the pease council, Roumania again declares war on Germany. United States decides to feed the German people. United States stops draft boards and lifts war restriction of industries. **Nov. 13**—American troops cross the German former frontier and enter Alsace-Lorraine.

November 14—Polish troops occupy the royal palaces in Warsaw and seize telegraph and telephone connections with Vienna. United States loans another hundred million dollars to Italy for food supplies. Dangerous bolshevik disorders in Germany and Austria. German crown prince interned in Holland.

November 15—Distinguished Service Medal conferred on General Pershing at his headquarters in France by General Tasker H. Bliss. United States Postoffice department takes control of all ocean cable lines, consent of other governments having been obtained. Prof. Thomas G. Masaryk proclaimed President of the new Czecho-Slav republic.

November 16—Copenhagen reported many German ships due for surrender under armistice conditions. Demobilization of United States troops ordered by the government, beginning with those in army camps at home. United States takes over express service. Belgian troops enter Brussels. German cruiser Wiesbaden torpedoed by German revolutionary sailors, with loss of 330 lives.

November 17—Two hundred and fifty thousand American troops advance nine miles in French territory evacuated by Germans. French armies advance across the west boundary of Alsace-Lorraine and occupy many towns. People of Luxemburg demand abdication of Grand Duchess.

November 18—President Wilson decides to attend the peace conference to be held in Europe. French occupy Metz. American troops reach the German border. Britsh troops land at Gallipoli. American troops defeat bolshevik forces at Fulka, on the river Dvina. United States government takes over German insurance companies' agencies in America to be sold by the Custodian of alien property.

November 29—The President announced names of commissioners to represent the United States at peace conference. They are: Woodrow Wilson, President of the United States; Robert Lansing, Secretary of State; Col. Edward M. House; Henry White, former ambassador to Italy and to France, and Gen. Tasker H. Bliss, American adviser of the supreme war council.

December 4, 1918—President Wilson and a numerous staff sailed for Europe from New York aboard the George Washington, escorted by warships under command of Admiral Mayo, to attend the Peace Conference at Versailles, France.